WOMEN IN SOCIETY

EGYPT

ANGÈLE BOTROS SAMAAN

MARSHALL CAVENDISH
New York • London • Sydney

Reference edition published 1993 by
Marshall Cavendish Corporation
2415 Jerusalem Avenue
P.O. Box 587
North Bellmore
New York 11710

© Times Editions Pte Ltd 1993

Originated and designed by
Times Books International, an imprint of
Times Editions Pte Ltd

Printed in Singapore

Cover picture by Christine Osborne

Library of Congress Cataloging-in-Publication Data:
Sam' an, Anzhil Butrus.
    Women in society. Egypt / Angele Botros Samaan.
    p. cm. — (Women in society)
    Includes bibliographical references and index.
    Summary: Examines the experiences of women
in Egyptian society, discussing their participation in
various fields and profiling the lives of significant
women.
    ISBN 1–85435–505–8 :
    1. Women—Egypt—Social conditions—Juvenile
literature.
    [1. Women—Egypt. 2. Egypt—Social conditions.]
I. Title.
II. Series: Women in society (New York, N.Y.)
HQ1793.S27 1992
305.42' 0962—dc20   92–12373
                                                      CIP
                                                       AC

Women in Society

Editorial Director	Shirley Hew
Managing Editor	Shova Loh
Editors	Goh Sui Noi
	Roseline Lum
	June Khoo Ai Lin
	Debra Fernando
	MaryLee Knowlton
	Junia Baker
	Sue Sismondo
Picture Editor	Nancy Yong
Production	Edmund Lam
Design	Tuck Loong
	Ong Su Ping
	Ang Siew Lian
Illustrations	Eric Siow/AC Graphic

Introduction

This book examines the role and status of women in Egyptian society. The woman is viewed both as wife and mother, and as participant in public life. Her place in the family has always been respected and revered. Outside the home, her role varied from time to time. As far back as Pharaonic times, the Egyptian woman, both as worker and queen, worked side by side with the man. Later, there were times of seclusion (the confining of women in the home) and regression, mainly under foreign domination. Social, religious, economic and political factors, throughout history, have had their impact on society in general and women's status in particular.

With the beginning of modern times, movements for national independence and social development were accompanied by demands for women's emancipation. Liberal thinkers and reformers paved the way and pioneer feminist activists soon joined in the fray. Programs for the advancement of women were repeatedly developed. They called basically for improvement in the areas of education, employment and family laws. As time went on, substantial changes were achieved.

In the course of this book, both group and individual roles of women in Egypt will be discussed. Examples of eminent and dynamic women from different walks of life will be highlighted.

Contents

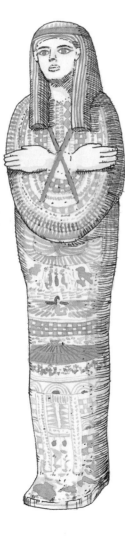

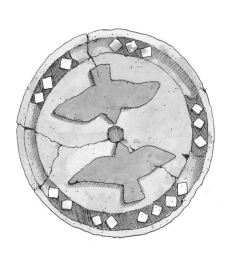

chapter one

The *Isis* Myth

sis ("ee-sis") was first worshiped in the Nile Delta. She was regarded as the sky goddess, who gave birth to the sun god once every day. She was one of the four children of Ged and Nut, god and goddess of the earth and the sky. The other three were Osiris, Set and Nephtys ("nef-tis"). Isis became wife to her eldest brother, King Osiris. Her sister Nephtys married Set, according to a Pharaonic tradition, to keep the royal blood in the family.

Osiris the "Good One," Isis the "Doer of All Good"

The temple of Isis at Philae (*opposite*) and Isis as she is often depicted in Egyptian drawings (*right*). Isis is one of the most loved and revered women in the history of ancient Egypt.

Osiris was a good king. He cared for his people and taught them the art of agriculture, how to fashion tools, grow corn and grapes, and make bread and wine. He built towns and issued just laws, and came to be known as the "Good One." As queen, Isis was her husband's right arm. She assisted in his civilizing projects. She taught the women how to bake bread, weave and make wicker baskets. As a result, she was named the "Doer of All Good."

Not content with civilizing his own people, Osiris set out to spread civilization to the rest of the world, leaving his beloved wife as regent. In his absence Isis governed wisely. When he returned, he found everything in perfect order.

Above: Isis (*left*) and Osiris (*right*). Isis represents for the Egyptians the loving and faithful wife, the caring and supportive mother, and the good and wise queen.

Opposite: Isis is often shown as a woman suckling her baby.

Conflict begins

The good Osiris soon fell prey to the plotting of his treacherous brother, Set. To get rid of Osiris and replace him on the throne, Set invited his brother to a banquet. Having had a beautifully-decorated chest made to fit his brother's size, he declared to his guests that the chest would be given to whom it fitted. When Osiris lay in the chest, to see if it fitted him, the box was firmly closed by Set's attendants and thrown into the Nile.

Isis, though distracted with worry and grief, set out to search for her husband. The search was long, but she finally found his body. With her magical powers she restored it to life. Osiris appeared before the tribunal of gods which returned him his throne. But he preferred to return to the Elysian Fields of the other world.

Isis, mother of Horus

After the birth of Horus, Isis was revered as "Mother of Horus." Protecting her son from the violent Set until he would be able to avenge his father and regain the throne became her sole aim. She hid him in the Delta marshes. When he was secretly poisoned by Set, she rescued him.

When Horus appeared before the tribunal to prove the justice of his cause, Isis used all womanly and magical powers for the purpose. She transformed herself alternately into an old woman, a beautiful damsel and a kite. She tricked Set into admitting Horus's right to the throne. Consequently, Horus came to be known as "Son of Isis."

In a song Isis is described as "she of the quick and sharp tongue, who utters no word in vain, and who is skillful in leadership."

The Isis myth

Origins of ancient myths, the Isis myth included, are often vague and inconsistent. One reason for this is that there are many sources. Another is the fact that ancient Egyptian religion was a rather creative religion, in the sense that as time passed, ritual was subject to revision. Most important, perhaps, is how long the Egyptian religion prevailed. The worship of Isis lasted from about the middle of the third millennium B.C. to the middle of the 6th century A.D. Furthermore, her worship was practiced in Egypt, Asia Minor and in parts of Europe.

Origins of her legend have survived in some of the countless Egyptian religious texts, containing references to mythological stories. Like such mythological accounts elsewhere, these stories were also handed down from one generation to another by word of mouth. Hence the inconsistencies. Thus the Osiris-Isis myth has survived in more than one version, and not always in complete form. Different versions stress different aspects of the myth, but the main line of action has been preserved.

Mother of all

Because of her loving nature, Isis won the title "Mother of All" and her defense of justice earned her the title "Goddess of Justice." She was also associated with fertility. It was believed that her tears for her husband caused the Nile flooding which watered the land. According to Herodotus, a Greek historian, she was revered by every inhabitant of Egypt. Nowadays, Isis is a common name among Egyptian women.

Outside Egypt, Isis came to be regarded as "Universal Mother." She was identified with Greek goddesses. Her temple in Philae, near Aswan in Upper Egypt, was built by the Ptolomies, and the Romans built temples for her in and near Rome.

Mirror of womanhood

Isis is mainly represented as a woman suckling her baby. Her statues, in stone, glass or gold, are scattered in museums all over the world. Her most recent statue was sculpted by the great Egyptian artist Mahmoud Mokhtar.

As far back as 3400 B.C., songs and prayers were written for Isis. In recent times, Tawfiq al-Hakim, the eminent Egyptian writer, published in 1955 a brilliant play, *Isis*. He depicted her both as a dedicated wife and mother and a pioneering woman seeking justice and the welfare of her people.

Though not all Egyptian women are expected to undertake all the roles she played, they are inspired by her example to attempt some of them.

chapter two

*M*ilestones

The history of women in Egypt, not unlike that in many other countries in the world, has been one of ups and downs. During periods of progress and enlightenment, the woman enjoyed a high status and readily played her role in society. At times of regression, she suffered a loss in status and her role in society was diminished. Throughout Egyptian history, the woman seems to have valued her role as wife and mother. She loved her husband, cared for her children and managed the household. She also actively participated in public life. She stood side by side with the men in times of peace and war. But when she felt that she was deprived of her rights as a human being, she rebelled, calling for freedom, justice, and equal opportunity.

Women in ancient Egypt: A golden age

Egypt is known to have had one of the oldest and most illustrious civilizations of the ancient world. Socially, economically and politically, ancient Egyptians enjoyed a good life. They had an established form of government thousands of years before Christianity, as their records richly testify.

Their enlightened view of life is reflected in their attitude toward women. They respected, revered and worshiped them. Their attitude is typical of early agricultural civilizations. The woman was associated with the land, its products and the cycle of life. Like Isis, other ancient Egyptian goddesses were revered for such associations. They came to be worshiped as time went on by the Greeks and the Romans.

Two ancient goddesses (*opposite*) and two modern women of Egypt (*right*). Through history, women in Egypt have experienced times of freedom and seclusion, but they have always fought for their rights.

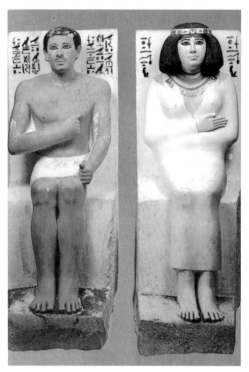

considering. A woman had the right to choose her husband. The husband had to promise in the marriage contract to treat his wife well and that she would be "part of himself," that is, as dear to him as himself.

Marriage and women Normally a husband had one wife and despite the use of the term *snt* ("snet"), meaning sister, to refer to a wife, it was seldom that a man actually married his sister. However, members of the royal family, especially kings, sometimes married their sisters, as in the case of Osiris and Isis, and Set and Nephtys, in order to keep the royal blood in the family.

Egyptians married early and adultery was frowned upon. If a wife was infertile, chronically ill or beyond child-bearing age, a man could marry more than one

Statues of a man and his wife, side by side. Many statues and drawings of ancient Egypt show men and women side by side, sometimes even with arms around each other.

The ancient Egyptians left records not only of their deities and kings and queens but of everyday life on the walls of their temples and tombs, on stones and papyrus. These were often accompanied by beautiful drawings which have largely been preserved. According to such records, women in ancient Egypt were greatly respected in the home and visibly active outside it. The family has always been of great importance to the Egyptian people. Hence the wealth of material on woman as wife.

The status of women as far back as the middle of the third millennium before Christ (2400 B.C.) is worth

A wise man, Tohotep, gave this piece of advice to men regarding women:

"If you become a man of great position, set up a house for her, and love your wife as seems right: give her food and clothe her and prepare oil for her, as it is a cure for the organs of her body. Don't argue with her, for she will not be violent, if you are gentle with her."

woman. He would depict them all with their names on the wall of his tomb. However, marrying more than one woman seems to have been rare. Divorce also was permitted, with the wife entitled to compensation unless she was found unfaithful.

Ancient Egyptian law was kind to the woman. She was regarded as equal to the man. In marriage, the man gave his wife two-thirds of his property. She was allowed to keep the share she brought with her from her own family and she could do what she liked with her property.

Women and society Outside the home, the ordinary woman worked in the field and in early forms of industry, with her husband or on her own. The Egyptian woman has through the ages shown a special skill for weaving and basket-making. She went to the market with the products of her industry, buying and selling goods. Women went hunting with their husbands, attended parties and enjoyed the pleasures of dancing, singing and music.

They also played an important part in religious life. There were goddesses to whom sacrifices were made and for whom marvelous festivals were held. They included the goddesses of justice, of the fields, of harvest, of heaven and of writing, as well as of love, beauty and fidelity. There were groups of priest-esses and singers in the temples that played music as part of worship.

Women of ancient Egypt went to the marketplace to buy and sell goods; they still do today.

Queen Nefertiti, wife of the Pharoah Akhenaten.

were marked by justice, progress, and stability.

A good example is Queen Hatshepsut of the 18th dynasty (1552–1306 B.C.). She restored greatness to the Egyptian empire by helping to free the country from the harsh and cruel Hyksos invaders.

In Pharaonic Egypt women began to have the privileges enjoyed only by kings since the sixth dynasty (2325–2125 B.C.). The queen, being the daughter, wife or mother of a god-king, had a distinguished status as part of the structure of the state, as well as great influence. The beautiful Queen Nefertiti, Akhenaten's wife, helped her husband to convert the people to the worship of one god, Aton, god of the sun. Queen Nefertari, another well-known Egyptian queen, helped her husband Ramses II (1290–1224 B.C.) during the 19th dynasty, in his campaigns against the enemies of Egypt.

Women and politics The ancient Egyptian woman occupied an eminent position in politics and government. She sat on the throne. Men were willing to be ruled by queens, who exercised power in their own right. Their reigns

> The ancient Egyptian's attitude toward women is reflected in their artistic representations. Egyptian kings are hardly seen without their wives beside them. If there is a statue of the husband on one side of a building, there will be another of his wife on the other.

Historical chronology

4000–3500 B.C.	The birth of civilization in Egypt.
2650–1551	Ancient and Middle kingdoms.
1650–1540	Hyksos rule.
1550–525	The New Kingdom marks the zenith of Pharaonic Egypt. The kingdom becomes a great trading and military power. Decline sets in after 1070.
525–30	Periods of Pharaonic rule interrupted by periods of foreign rule, including Assyrian, Persian, Macedonian, and Ptolemic.
30 B.C.–A.D. 640	Roman rule.
640–660	Egypt conquered by the Arabs. Arabic becomes the main language and Islam the main religion.
660–1250	Ummayad, Fatimid and Ayyubid rule.
1250–1517	Mamluks rule over Egypt.
1517	Egypt becomes part of the Turkish Ottoman Empire.
1798–1801	French Occupation.
1805–1848	Modern Egypt founded by Mohamad Ali.
1869	Suez Canal is opened.
1882–1914	British Occupation. Orabi Rebellion takes place in 1882.
1914	World War I breaks out. Egypt is made a protectorate of Britain.
1922	Egypt gains independence, but the British assert strong influence under the constitutional monarchy.
1952	In a coup in July, army officers led by Abdel Nasser remove King Farouk from the throne. Egypt becomes a republic under one-party rule.
1954	Nasser becomes president.
1956	Egypt takes possession of the Suez Canal. The country is invaded by Israel, Britain and France, but world opinion forces foreign troops to withdraw. A new constitution gives women the vote.
1957	First parliamentary elections contested by women. Two women win seats.
1962	The National Charter. First woman minister appointed.
1967	Israel launches a surprise attack on Egypt and achieves a quick victory.
1971	A new constitution for Egypt is approved by referendum, which allows for a multi-party system of government.
1973	Fourth Egypt–Israel war.
1979	Egypt and Israel sign peace treaty. Sinai is returned to Egypt.
1981	President Sadat is assassinated, Mohamad Hosni Mubarak is elected president.
1987	Egypt restores ties with the Arab world.
1991	Egyptian forces take part in the Gulf War. Dr. Boutros Boutros Ghali is elected United Nations General Secretary.

Under the yoke of invaders

A battle between Roman and Egyptian soldiers. After the Pharaonic rule, Egypt came under the domination of different foreign aggressors for several centuries.

Ramses III (1182–1151 B.C.) was the last of the great Pharaohs. He was succeeded by weak kings and the Egyptian empire was soon in decline. Then for a number of centuries, except for short periods of varying lengths, Egypt was the coveted prey of foreign rising empires.

Owing to its strategic position at the juncture of three continents and on commercial and military routes, it came under the domination of powers of different cultures: Assyrians, Persians, Greeks, and Romans. However, this did not greatly disrupt the basic Egyptian lifestyle, especially regarding family and the status of women. On the contrary, many of these foreign invaders adapted to Egyptian ways of life, even worshiping the local deities.

The invaders used the resources of the country for their own economic gain and for military purposes, and left its people to carry on with their own ways. Except for imposed laws on matters of tributes and property, which naturally left their mark on the economy, the social structure remained more or less unchanged.

Nevertheless, some of these periods of foreign rule were good for the country. Under Ptolemic rule, Egypt became a "brilliant kingdom" again, and a Greek-Egyptian culture emerged.

Queen Cleopatra

The famed Queen Cleopatra was the Ptolemic ruler who ruled Egypt from 51 to 30 B.C. Although Greek in origin, she was often regarded as Egyptian. She thought of Egypt as her home and country. She is remembered as a queen who cared for the welfare of Egypt and struggled to preserve the entity and unity of the country.

The Romans had gained a foothold in Egypt, in Alexandria, at the same time that Cleopatra became queen, and she found herself involved in Roman politics.

Later she married the Roman Mark Antony, one of Julius Caesar's heirs. After Caesar's death, there was a struggle for power between Antony and his rival Octavius. Cleopatra joined in the fray on the side of Antony. In the naval battle of Actium in 31 B.C., the fleets of Antony and Cleopatra were defeated. In the eyes of successive generations, her defeat is atoned for by her bravely taking her own life rather than being taken captive by Octavius.

Cleopatra's life and death is celebrated in an Arabic poetic play, *The Death of Cleopatra*. She is presented as a brave and able woman who utters these passionate words:

"I die as I lived for the throne of Egypt
For it I give up the throne of beauty."

The Hanging Church in Cairo. Christianity came to Egypt during the 1st century A.D.

Advent of Christianity

The advent of Christianity in Egypt occurred, according to tradition, some time during the reign of the Roman emperor Nero (A.D. 54–68). It spread through Egypt within half a century. Christianity found fertile soil in Egypt. It is particularly associated with the story of the flight of the Holy Family to Egypt and with St. Mark the Evangelist's sojourn in Alexandria. The lifestyle of the Copts, as the Egyptian Christians came to be called—"Copt" being the corrupted Greek word for "Egyptian"—was based on the Christian principles of love, justice, equality and service to others. According to Christian teaching, the woman is the man's helpmate, to be cared for and cherished. A man can only have one wife and divorce is very rare.

Persecution As time went on, Egypt became a stronghold of Orthodox Christianity. The Copts, in later years, steadfastly withstood Roman attempts to turn them away from the new religion back to pagan gods. Among those who suffered persecution and death rather than give up their faith were some brave women, whose names have endured.

St. Damiana, a beautiful young woman, who refused marriage and dedicated herself to the service of God and the surrounding community, was put to death, together with 40 virgins, at the orders of Emperor Diocletian. Another woman, known to all as "The Mother of Five," was subjected to the agony of witnessing her five sons being brutally tortured, and died as a result. Both are examples of Egyptian women's fortitude.

Islamic influences

The Arab conquest of Egypt (A.D. 640)

occurred at a time when Roman rule was at its harshest and most despotic. The Egyptians were not inclined to resist the new invaders, who soon established themselves in the country. Moslem rule had a great impact on life in general and on women in particular. Islam aimed at developing laws and traditions to free humanity and establish justice for all human beings. It preached equality of the sexes regarding rights and duties, education, work, religion, and government.

In principle, the gain for women was to be both social and economic: Islam entitled women to ownership of their own independent fortune. They could dispose of it, trade with it, or bequeath it to someone other than their heirs. They could engage in business, and provide a guarantee or grant donations in their own names.

Saint Verena

St. Verena, a native of Garagoz, a town near Thebes, now Luxor, is venerated not only in Egypt but also in Switzerland. As a young woman, together with other nurses, she accompanied a legion sent by Emperor Diocletian to quell a rebellion in Gaul, part of which is now Switzerland. When the members of the legion, Christians all, refused to pay homage to the Roman god before battle, they were ruthlessly killed, but the nurses were spared.

Verena decided to remain in Gaul and dedicated her life to educating the people there to become Christians and teaching them the principles of hygiene. On the site where she was buried, one church after another was built in her name by the people of Zurich. She has become the Patron Saint of Housewives and the Healer of Lepers in Switzerland.

The first mosque in Egypt, the Amr mosque, in Cairo. Islam came to Egypt with the Arab conquest of the country in A.D. 640.

Women in a teaching circle at the al-Azhar mosque, the oldest Islamic school in Egypt.

Opposite: Mamluk tombs in the City of the Dead. The Mamluks left behind beautiful and magnificent buildings.

Marriage Moslem women could accept or refuse a marriage proposal. Husbands had to give adequate financial support to their wives, even if the wives were themselves wealthy. After marriage, a Moslem woman kept her own property which she had brought with her. In case of divorce, Islam safeguarded a woman's financial and moral rights. Much of this was reminiscent of ancient Egyptian marriage arrangements.

Islam is often associated in non-Moslem minds with polygamy and easy divorce. It should be pointed out that the right to have more than one wife was restricted to a condition almost impossible to humanly fulfill, and that is, the husband had to treat all the wives equally in every way.

Divorce too was allowed only in case of necessity. In practice, however, these principles were often forgotten and women suffered, especially at times of regression and decadence. Divorce was easier for the man than for the woman. A wife had to go to court if her husband refused to divorce her, unless it was stated in the marriage contract that she had the right to divorce him. A Moslem man could divorce his wife by just telling her "You are divorced." This had to be registered by a Mazoun ("MAH-zon," an official who registers marriages and divorces.)

Marriage is often subject to custom and tradition. Under Moslem rule, as in almost all periods of foreign rule, Copts followed the Christian rules of marriage to one wife. As time went on, family laws, or personal status laws as they came to be called, were one of the main issues of the women's emancipation movement in Egypt.

Shagaret el-Dorr During the Moslem period, education was not available to all women. However, there were chances for women to be educated. One educated woman who showed competence in managing the affairs of the country was Shagaret el-Dorr (Pearl Tree), the first woman sultan of Egypt.

During the last stage of the Crusades, around 1249, during the absence of her husband the sultan, and later after his death, she acted first as regent, then as sultan in her own right.

According to some versions, it was through her marriage to Aybak, one of the Mamluk army officers who played a leading role in defeating the French Crusaders, that Egypt fell under the rule of the Mamluks, which lasted from 1260 to 1517. During the Ottoman period that followed, the Mamluks continued to be a powerful class, until the beginning of the 19th century when Mohamad Ali, generally known as the founder of modern Egypt, finally expelled them in 1811.

The Mamluk era

This era was not a happy one for the people of Egypt. The rulers were far less concerned with the people they ruled than with personal interests, wealth, and military glory. The people were useful only for providing the work force and money in the form of taxes. It was also a period of instability and continuous struggles for power.

The whole population, including women, suffered. Apart from the pampered wives of the Mamluks themselves, very little is known of any Egyptian women making a mark on history. What the Mamluks left behind is a wealth of beautiful and magnificent buildings in the form of mosques and hospitals, which can still be seen in the older parts of Cairo.

The Mamluks

The Mamluks were originally slaves of non-Arab stock—Turkish, Circassian or Mongolian—whom the caliphs and sultans of the Arab world acquired as bodyguards and soldiers from the 10th century onward.

Later, when their services became indispensable, they were freed, and many of them were appointed to high army positions. As time went on, they became so powerful that they challenged the existence of their rulers, originally their masters. Thus the Arab rule ended and the Mamluks' started.

Turkish rule

Turkish rule (1517–1798) under the Ottoman dynasty was even more despotic and disastrous for Egypt than that of the Mamluks. Socially, economically and politically, it was a period of regression.

For women, it was a period of confinement. Aspects of women's seclusion, such as the harem (women's quarters) and the veil (covering for the head and/or face), are generally associated with the Ottoman lifestyle. They both existed in earlier ages, but the Ottoman rule brought the segregation of men and women to its highest point. In Turkey itself, restrictions on women increased as time went on. Women were given no education and hardly any legal rights.

In Egypt, as in most other countries under Turkish rule, there were times of regression, but also periods when women could obtain some education, and consequently a degree of freedom. It should also be pointed out that seclusion and the veil were urban customs not adopted by rural women.

The French occupation

The French occupation of Egypt lasted only three years, from 1798 to 1801. Despite what may have been cultural benefits for the country, by way of providing a window on the West, it was a period of foreign rule and as such grievous to the Egyptians, who were in constant rebellion against it. Foreign rule angered and humiliated the Egyptians. There were moments of both political and social significance, when they rebelled against such rule. Egypt's strong desire for freedom from occupation and exploitation was no less strong than its fervent longing for better social and economic conditions.

It is to the credit of Egyptian women that they participated at such moments. Egyptian women showed their fine mettle by joining in resistance activities. One memorable example is the 1798 Boulac and Rashid uprising against the French who were led by Napoleon. Women were out in the scene of conflict, not only to tend to the wounded, hand arms to the combatants, and carry equipment, but also to take part in the fray.

> **At times women actually used weapons to fight with the French, at others they hurled stones to stop French troops from advancing. When they could neither fight nor fetch and carry, they cheered and chanted to encourage the men. Such acts of bravery may have contributed to a heightened awareness of the need for reform where women were concerned.**

A national renaissance: Calls for reform

The emancipation of women in Egypt began with the modern age. The last third of the 19th century witnessed a national reawakening, a renaissance. This was reflected in a renewal of literature and the arts together with a demand for reform in all aspects of life, notably a reassessment of women's place in society. One of the pioneer thinkers to call for reform was Rifa'a al-Tahtawi (1801–1873).

Tahtawi on equal opportunities for women Tahtawi's book, *The True Guide for the Education of Girls and Boys* (1873), is a milestone in the movement for women's emancipation. For a long time, girls had been deprived of a true chance for education. This book was the initial step toward a long process which led to equal opportunities for women in the fields of education and work.

Tahtawi discussed the benefits of education in general and for women in particular. It would enhance women's moral and intellectual capabilities and make them more likely to seek knowledge. Moreover, with education, they would be equipped for participation in conversation and discussion of ideas with men, thus heightening their worth in their own eyes and improving their status, as they would be freed from light-heartedness and silliness.

Rifa'a al-Tahtawi, a pioneer in the women's emancipation movement in Egypt.

Tahtawi is also credited for being one of the earliest advocates of women's employment:

"When necessary, women can undertake of the work and occupation of men whatever agrees with their strength and energy. All that women can do, they should do themselves. Idle hands tend to promote idle talk and indulgence in gossip. Work protects the woman from improprieties and enhances her virtue. If idleness is a vice in men, it is a greater vice in women."

Qassim Amin, a man ahead of his time who believed that women should be economically independent if they were to escape the tyranny of their men.

The beginning of emancipation

The women's emancipation movement in Egypt grew in tandem with the process of national liberation. During the rebellion led by Ahmad Orabi in 1882, more advocates of women's rights appeared on the scene. Mohamad Abdou (1849–1905) wrote an article in 1881 calling for women's emancipation and for the restoration of the rights given to them by the Koran but suspended under Ottoman restrictions.

Abdulla al-Nadim, a great nationalist leader of the Orabi rebellion and writer, wrote a series of articles in dialogue form, entitled *The Girls' School*, in which he emphasized the need for women's education.

Qassim Amin The turn of the century witnessed the rise to fame of the most eminent advocates of the women's cause. Qassim Amin (1863–1908) argued that the way to political reform was through social and cultural reform, and social reform must include women's emancipation.

Qassim Amin was a passionate and persuasive writer and he devoted all his energies to the women's cause. He wrote two books which were published one immediately after the other: *The Liberation of Woman* (1899) and *The New Woman* (1900).

In the first book *The Liberation of Woman*, he wrote that the position of women could only be improved by education. Women should have sufficient schooling to enable them not only to manage their households properly, but more importantly, to equip them to earn their living. He thus anticipated the modern idea of women's economic independence. He believed that education was the only sure guarantee of women's rights. Unless a woman could support herself she would always be at the mercy of male tyranny, no matter what rights the laws gave her. She would then have to secure power for herself by devious means. Education would not only end tyranny, but also the veiling and seclusion of women.

Amin thought that women's problems could be solved by prohibiting the right to have more than one wife and restricting divorce except for extreme necessity. He was careful to point out that these views were consistent with the teachings of the Koran and the Shari'a (Islamic Law). Nevertheless, according to records, Amin's book aroused a storm. In the few months after its publication it gave rise to a series of books and pamphlets, some attacking, some supporting his thesis. In reply to his critics, Amin published a second book on the subject of the new woman. In part, it is a new statement of the ideas in the first, but its tone is very different.

In his second book, *The New Woman*, Amin went as far as to say that legislation concerning women should lead to their participation in all posts of government, including political rights. These views took more than half a century to bear fruit. However, Qassim Amin had lit a torch.

Lutfi al-Sayyed Lutfi al-Sayyed (1872–1963), a liberal thinker, government official, educator, university professor and rector, not only canvassed for women's rights but had a hand in implementing at least one of them, the right to education. As editor of an influential paper, *al-Jarida* (*The Newspaper*) and member of a political party, he assisted in founding the Egyptian University in 1908. Later, in 1928, he admitted the first Egyptian women into the university.

He maintained that education should aim at creating a nation morally and mentally united around the modern sciences and the principles implied in them. More important than the education given in the schools was that given in the family. The welfare of the family was the welfare of the nation, and the problem of the Egyptian family was at the heart of the problem of Egypt. In the upper and middle classes the main problem was the seclusion of women— in other words, their inequality with men. Two things then were necessary: the emancipation of women and their education.

Lutfi al-Sayyed, an educator who helped found the Egyptian University in 1908 and later admitted the first Egyptian women into the university, in 1928.

Time for struggle

One of the first women activists of the early 20th century was Malak Hifni Nassif (1886–1918), generally known as Bahithat al-Badiyah (Searcher of the Desert). She was the first Egyptian woman to obtain a primary school certificate and later a teacher's certificate.

She taught, wrote articles for newspapers and magazines, and lectured at the Egyptian University as part of a free course.

She was the first Egyptian woman to attend and speak at the National Assembly, the first Egyptian legislative council in modern times, in 1911. She submitted to the Assembly a 10-point program on women's development, historically known as the first formulation of its kind. The following are the most important demands:

- Girls should be educated in the Koran and the Shari'a (Islamic Law).
- There should be primary and secondary education for girls and compulsory primary education for all classes of people, whether rich or poor.
- Some girls should be allowed to pursue a complete course in medical studies and in methods of teaching, to meet the needs of all women in Egypt.
- Girls should·be admitted to any branch of higher studies they choose.
- The Moslem legal process of engagement, that two people should not get engaged before having met in the presence of an adult, should be followed.
- Polygamy and divorce should be subject to a judge's approval.

Unfortunately, all these demands were rejected.

Malak died on October 21, 1918, and her body was wrapped in the national flag in recognition of her services to the country and its women. The traditional Egyptian commemoration ceremony that pays homage to the deceased 40 days after death, was held at the Egyptian University.

Political leaders and women's emancipation The political leaders were no less in favor of the emancipation of women. Though more publicly concerned with issues of national liberation, they did support women's emancipation. Mustafa Kamel (1874–1908), a nationalist leader, used to ask educated women to read his letters at public gatherings which he could not personally attend. Saad Zaghloul ("sahd ZAG-lool," 1860–1928), leader of the Wafd Party, for some time sympathized with the activists of the first two feminist organizations: the Committee for Wafdist Women and the Egyptian Feminist Union. Later he became rather conservative.

Literary salon As early as 1888, Princess Nazli Fadil, an outstanding woman of culture, organized a literary salon, the first of its kind in the East. It was frequented by writers, thinkers and reform activists. Among those who attended it were Mohamad Abdou, Qassim Amin and Saad Zaghloul. It has even been said that Amin had opposed women's emancipation until he was taken to the salon by a friend. His meeting with Nazli Fadil made him change his mind.

The 1919 revolution

With the end of World War I, it was time for the British forces, which had occupied Egypt since 1882, to keep their promise regarding self-determination, and depart. When signs indicated that they intended to stay, nationalist leaders took action. With the aborted Orabi Rebellion (1882) still fresh in the Egyptian memory, the 1919 Revolution, led by Saad Zaghloul, roused the whole nation, men and women, to more forceful action. When Zaghloul, as leader of the Wafd (Delegation) Party, was refused permission to go to England to plead Egypt's cause, there were strikes and demonstrations by all sectors of society. Four of the party leaders were exiled and this triggered an uprising.

Princess Nazli Fadil, an outstanding woman who organized a literary salon which was frequented by writers, thinkers and reformers.

Women demonstrate in the streets of Cairo March 20, 1919, was to be a major milestone in the history of Egyptian women's struggle for their rights. A group of veiled women led by Hoda Shaarawi (1879–1947), wife of one of the exiled men, mounted an unprecedented demonstration in the streets of Cairo to protest the British occupation of Egypt. Though it was a peaceful demonstration, some women were wounded and the first modern woman political martyr was killed by British soldiers.

Her funeral was the clarion bell that spurred Egyptian women to rally in a 300-woman demonstration, to file a protest with the British Commissioner. This second women's demonstration is said to have really triggered the revolution throughout Egypt.

This militant participation in the national uprising not only proved women's ability to play an active role in the affairs of their country, but marked an important step forward along the path to freedom.

Committee for Wafdist Women

Soon after the women's demonstrations, the Committee for Wafdist Women was established on January 8, 1920. Like their leader, Hoda Shaarawi, the members were mainly educated women of the upper class, all devoted to their

Veiled women demonstrators who took to the streets in 1919 to protest the continued occupation of Egypt by British forces after World War I.

country's cause. A central committee was elected to formulate the Committee's aims, which reflected the kind of political activity the Committee was planning to engage in.

The aim of the central committee was to convey to the main Wafd Party the aspirations of Egyptian women and their intention to seek, as much as possible, Egypt's complete independence.

The Committee addressed an open letter to the British authorities. Other letters of protests were sent in due course to the Prime Minister, to the central committee of the Wafd Party and to newspapers. This was a protest against the British forces' attack on peaceful demonstrations and on the continuation of martial law. To confirm its active role, the Committee participated in as many nationalist activities as possible, protesting when not consulted on an issue and freely giving an opinion when it was.

In March 1923 the Committee received the first invitation from the International Alliance of Women to attend a conference in Rome in May 1923. This was a welcome sign of international appreciation of Egyptian women's activism. A delegation of three members, who were to leave their mark on the women's movement—Hoda Shaarawi, Nabawiyya Moussa (1886–1951) and Ceza Nabarawi (1897–1985)—were chosen to attend.

Egyptian Feminist Union

For the first time Egyptian women's voice was to be heard at an international gathering. A result of this invitation was the establishment of the Egyptian Feminist Union on March 16, 1923. The Egyptian delegation to the Rome conference would be representing the Union.

Two articles of the Union constitution were:

- The aim of the Union is to raise the woman's intellectual and social standard to the degree that would qualify her to have the same rights and duties as the man.
- The Union will pursue all legal means for the woman's attaining her political rights.

Hoda Shaarawi (*left*) and Ceza Nabarawi, two pioneer feminists who attended the 1923 Rome conference of the International Alliance of Women.

The most memorable outcome of the Rome conference occurred when the ship that brought the three delegates home from Rome docked in Alexandria. In full sight of all those awaiting them, Hoda, followed by the others, took off her veil and threw it in the Mediterranean. This act was regarded as outrageous. Hoda's husband, who was among the waiting crowd, was embarrassed by his wife's "scandalous" behavior and divorced her. But they later remarried. However high the price paid, this was a glorious enactment of a long-cherished dream.

The Rome Conference The Egyptian delegation's participation in the Rome conference was both successful and colorful. Hoda Shaarawi proudly told the story of the welcome the delegates received and the interest they aroused. The Egyptian flag, carrying a cross and a crescent, symbolizing the unity of the Moslems and Christians of Egypt, was hoisted on the platform opposite that of the host country, because Egypt was the oldest country represented at the conference.

As a result of the Union's participation in the Rome conference, the Union was accorded membership in the International Alliance of Women.

Political activities Hoda Shaarawi drew up an ambitious statement of the Union's objectives regarding the demand for equal political rights for women. It comprised most of the earlier demands formulated by men and women advocates of women's rights.

Later a more modest and practical statement was drawn up by the Union, and submitted by a small delegation to the Prime Minister. It demanded, among other things, that women be admitted to secondary and higher education, and that the legal age of 16 for marriage for girls should be set.

The Union also campaigned against legalized prostitution. Politically, the Union issued statements whenever it disagreed with current policies or felt a protest against certain policies was needed.

Welfare program The Union started a welfare venture: a school in one of the popular districts to teach women the principles of hygiene and nursing and also some handicraft. Another function was to treat sick women and children. In keeping with the tradition of social work in Egypt, both the Union members and the doctors who took part in this welfare venture were volunteers.

As time went on, two issues came to be widely regarded as central to feminist activism: education for women and legal protection regarding marriage and divorce. Other issues, work for women, unveiling and women's participation in political life, were on the agenda, but came second to women's intellectual and social advancement.

Women admitted to the university

Taha Hussain (1889–1973) was a blind village boy who became a distinguished scholar, writer and later minister of education. He left his mark on many aspects of education in Egypt, including the admittance of women to university. According to Hoda Shaarawi's memoirs, this is how he revealed how the first 17 women were admitted to the Egyptian University:

"I think that the fact that I no longer hold an official position allows me to unravel to you a very serious 'conspiracy' contrived some years ago. The conspirators were a group of university men. They plotted among themselves to deceive the government and deprive it of one of its rights: the right to admit or not to admit women to the Egyptian University....but for this 'conspiracy'...which was hatched behind closed doors, it would not have been possible for us and for the Feminist Union to present to you an Egyptian lawyer and four women literary scholars today. These men agreed among themselves to confront the ministry of education with the accomplished act. The university rules allowed admission of Egyptians without specifying whether male or female. Thus, we plotted to accept young women if they applied for admission, and as they had applied, we just admitted them and told no one about it. Only when the act was accomplished did the ministry come to know that women had joined the Egyptian University."

University education for women

Why education was regarded as the first priority will be better understood when the situation of schools is clarified. The first government primary school for girls was established in 1873. The first secondary school followed only in 1921, but it did not qualify girls for the secondary school certificate. Some private schools already existed.

The first primary school for girls was founded by the Coptic patriarch, Kirolos IV, in 1855, and was attended by Christian and Moslem girls. There were some foreign missionary schools, and rich families' daughters were tutored at home. In both urban and rural areas, there were one-class schools that taught the Koran, reading, writing and arithmetic, for both boys and girls.

Despite a certain degree of controversy and opposition, change was accelerated. A regular secondary school was opened in 1925. As the first girls obtained their secondary school certificate, the more thorny issue of university education had to be resolved.

Determined to gain admittance despite opposition, a group of girls went to see the rector of the Egyptian University, Lutfi al-Sayyed, a strong advocate of women's education. As a result the girls were admitted without too much publicity. A number of these women have become eminent figures.

After the first 17 women were admitted to the university, other women were allowed to enter the university.

Members of the militant organization Daughter of the Nile on a hunger strike in 1954. They were agitating for women's right to vote. The new constitution of 1956 gave women the vote.

The struggle continues

Women have continued to push more visibly forward. On one front, a young Egyptian woman, Horreya Idris, an active feminist of the younger generation, won a beauty contest held in Lebanon, in 1934—a far cry from the days of the veil. On another, at the International Alliance of Women conference in 1935, Hoda Shaarawi was elected head of the Alliance with a majority vote of 148 out of 166, the first woman from the East to attain this position.

Between 1943 and 1945, a number of more militant women's organizations came into being. There were repeated attempts to achieve more of women's demands, but without much success.

Daughter of the Nile The years 1946–1952 were a period of unrest culminating in the 1952 Revolution which ended the monarchy and brought about many important changes in Egyptian life, some of which directly influenced women's status in society.

In 1941 Dorriyya Shafiq formed a militant organization, Bint el-Nil (Daughter of the Nile), which aimed at raising the standard of family life culturally, socially and hygienically, and sought to legalize measures to consolidate it. Unlike her predecessors, Dorriyya adopted more sensational methods to achieve her aims. In 1951 she and some followers occupied the parliament building, demanding women's representation. In 1954 they staged a hunger strike at the journalists' syndicate and threatened to fast to death unless the government gave women the vote in the new constitution that was being prepared.

Decades of achievement The new 1956 constitution did grant women the vote. Both the new constitution and the vote for women are firmly associated with Gamal Abdel Nasser's revolutionary government. In the elections of 1957, a number of women ran for office and two of them won seats in the new parliament, achieving a new victory.

In 1959 a law was issued against discrimination on the basis of sex.

The last few decades have witnessed unprecedented change regarding women's role and status in society, both by individuals and organizations. The struggle for greater advancement has continued, leading to real achievements. Landmarks have been the appointment of the first Egyptian woman minister and the first Egyptian woman ambassador, besides many appointments to high positions in government and universities. There have been also legal reforms in the areas of women's representation in parliament and, above all, in family law.

Two laws, in 1979 and 1985 respectively, imposed restrictions on easy divorce and polygamy. Facilities to help working women were made available by law. Egyptian women can be said to have attained equality in some areas of society.

> **The National Charter of 1962 states:**
> "Woman must be regarded as equal to man and must shed all the shackles that impede her from taking a constructive part in the national life."

Egyptian women today are still working toward the betterment of their lives, as well as the lives of their family.

chapter three

Women in Society

Women's contribution to the work force increased significantly in the second half of the 20th century as a result of the spread of education. This was accompanied by a degree of social and cultural change in the attitude toward women's work. Previously it was thought that work would interfere with a young woman's chance of a good marriage. Now a job is often regarded as an asset even among privileged classes. The economic factor is no longer the only incentive for working. Women find self-fulfillment in work.

Unpaid work, as a source of self-satisfaction, has always been part of a woman's life, whether in the home or as voluntary work outside it. Paid employment, seen in the context of women's emancipation, is a positive action for change. It is a manifestation of women's economic contribution to the family and society.

Besides participating in the traditional areas of education, health and social work, women have been gaining access to the areas of politics, business, technology, and scientific research.

Equal opportunity and equal pay are the general rule. However, discrimination based on sex exists in some areas.

In the last two decades, there has been a call for women to stay at home. Fundamentalist ideas and economic conditions have contributed to this. Still, the majority of young women want an education and a job.

Whether as policewoman in the city (*opposite*) or a farmer's wife in the country (*right*), women in Egypt contribute greatly to their society.

problem. The illiteracy rate among women has been slightly reduced in the last few decades. However, women still have a great deal of catching up to do. According to the 1986 Census, about 40% of females are literate as opposed to 60% of males.

Women in college The number of women attending college has been steadily increasing since 1928 when the first women were admitted to the Egyptian University. With 13 universities in Egypt now, college education is accessible to both men and women throughout the country.

College education is free on both undergraduate and graduate levels. No constraints are placed on the choice of subjects except marks obtained in the School Leaving Certificate examinations. Women made up 6% of college students in 1954. By the mid-1980s it was 34% for undergraduates and 33% for graduate students.

Teaching is a field in which women are found in large numbers. While in the past women teachers mainly taught in girls' schools, there are now many women teachers in boys' schools too.

Education

Combating illiteracy Though much has been achieved in the area of education among women, more remains to be done, especially among rural women and the less privileged urban groups. Illiteracy among a sizeable sector of these groups is a cause for concern.

As a Third World country, Egypt is exerting great efforts to deal with this

Teaching in the schools Education is a traditional field for women's employment.

Women teach not only in girls' and coeducational schools, but of late, in boys' schools too. Their numbers in the boys' schools have been increasing owing largely to the drop in the number of male teachers, as a result of temporary migration to the neighboring oil

Free education for all

Since the early feminists' demand for the improvement of women's education, progress has been achieved. Education is now free at all levels regardless of sex. Primary education was declared free in 1944, secondary education in 1950 and college education in 1962.

In 1956 primary education from the age of six to 12 became compulsory. Together with a more enlightened climate of opinion, this gradually resulted in an increase in the number of girls from all social classes attending school and college. Traditionally Egyptians, even those of the more privileged class, were more inclined to invest in the education of sons rather than daughters. In rural areas traditions prevented girls from continuing school after the age of 13 or 14. Early marriage also caused a high drop-out rate after primary school. Of late, however, there has been significant change in this area.

countries or to the cities to seek other employment.

Women have been promoted to positions of school head, inspector, dean of curriculum and under-secretaries for education.

Karima al-Said, a pioneer in education, started her career in 1932 as the first Egyptian woman to teach in a secondary school. In 1966 she became the first woman under-secretary for education. She was the first woman to be awarded the Order of the Republic, a medal awarded by the state for distinctive service.

Teaching in the universities In the universities women occupy all faculty ranks in increasing numbers. The numbers vary from one faculty to another and from one specialization to another. The number of women teaching in the universities is encouraging. In Cairo University, for instance, about one-third of the lecturers are women, while nearly a quarter of the professors are women.

Interestingly, the largest number of women professors are to be found in mass communications (50%) and medicine (33%), followed by dentistry, pharmacy, science, and economics. There are fewer women professors in commerce and engineering (only 18%).

For some time, women students were concentrated in the humanities, languages, science, medicine, and law. Later they joined the faculty of dentistry in 1932, commerce and pharmacy in 1935, engineering and agriculture in 1945. Veterinary medicine and the Arabic language faculties, male bastions for a long time, admitted women students in 1953.

Health and medicine

Nursing This is another accepted area for women's participation in the work force. In Egypt one of the earliest occupational schools as far back as 1831 was a school for midwives. This was followed by several nursing schools.

The Higher Institute of Nursing at Cairo University has produced highly trained nurses since the early '60s. Some of them pursue higher studies and a few have been awarded M.Sc. and Ph.D. degrees.

> Medicine is a demanding profession. It requires capability, dedication and time. The women who choose it are generally prepared to put up with all its responsibilities. Most of them manage to successfully undertake their dual roles as professionals and homemakers, despite enormous pressures.

Pioneer women doctors Among the first women to be sent to England to be educated in 1921, two became eminent doctors: Helana Sidaros and Kawkab Hifni Nassif. They both studied obstetrics and gynecology, this being the accepted branch for women at the time. Dr. Kawkab Hifni Nassif became the first Egyptian woman hospital director. Of the first group of Egyptian women to be admitted to the university, four studied medicine.

Contemporary women doctors The number of women medical students has since multiplied enormously. Many of the young women who achieve the best results in the School Leaving Certificate examinations choose to study medicine. Those who do well in their medical examinations are appointed to junior faculty posts, and eventually some of them reach professorial ranks. One of the highest percentages of women professors at Cairo University is in medicine.

Unlike the pioneers who practiced only obstetrics and gynecology, women doctors have ventured into nearly all branches of medicine, including surgery. Until recently this was a strongly-defended male area. The first woman to be awarded the M.D. degree in surgery by Cairo University in 1989 was widely regarded as a pioneer. Women excel in many specializations, such as pediatrics, ophthalmology, psychiatry, orthodontics, and clinical pathology.

Women doctors practice medicine in public and private hospitals. They are increasingly having their own private practices. Large numbers work for the Ministry of Health hospitals throughout the country.

The first blood bank Dr. Zeinab al-Sobki established the first blood bank in Egypt. She has been General Director of the Blood Bank of the Red Crescent

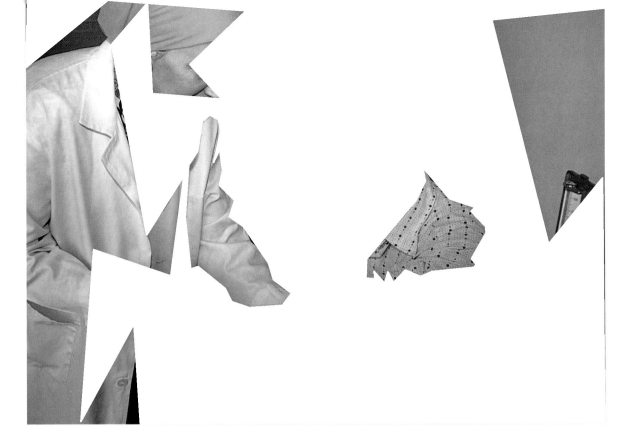

(equivalent of the Red Cross) since 1973, and of the Blood Bank of the Cairo University Hospital from 1953 to 1973.

Women in medical technology In the drug industry, women play a significant role. The entire work force in the manufacturing of contraceptive pills is female. Women, therefore, contribute in implementing one of the most urgent national projects. In a country where the problem of overpopulation is a cause of great social and economic worry, family planning is an area where women's participation is greatly appreciated. Another area where women's participation is dominant is that of the production of rehydration solution through a joint venture with the United Nations. Here it is mainly babies they save.

Science and technology

Women scientists have excelled particularly in the fields of university education and research. Six of the first women to go to the university studied science. Technology came later. It is one area in which women have contributed to national development. Egypt is one of the first Third World countries to use scientific and technological research for the purpose of development. Though rather recent, women's participation in this area is considerable.

Two women scientists, Samira Moussa and Tomader el-Khalafawi, have participated in atomic energy research.

Dr. Hanaa Mohammed, a doctor at the el-Taarof Medical Centre. Women doctors of today are venturing into other branches of medicine besides obstetrics and gynecology, the traditional field of medicine for them.

Social work

This is perhaps the oldest accepted field for women's activity outside the home. It is also one of the major areas of unpaid employment. Records of organized welfare work in Egypt date from the early years of this century. Nevertheless, efforts had certainly been exerted in this field much earlier.

A fund-raising bazaar. Women in Egypt, like women elsewhere, are the backbone of voluntary social work.

Social work in the 20th century owes its beginnings to the dynamic feminist pioneer, Hoda Shaarawi, and a number of upper-class, socially-motivated women. A major achievement in the field was made by Princess Ain al-Hayat, who got a group of women together to form a voluntary association to establish a day hospital in 1904. This later came to be called Mabarrat Mohamad Ali, one of the best hospitals in Cairo.

A group of women founded in 1909 the New Woman Association, and elected Hoda Shaarawi as honorary chairman. The association worked toward the advancement of women and undertook welfare work.

The efforts for women's emancipation went hand in hand with welfare work. At the time that Hoda Shaarawi and her colleagues were calling for the vote, among other political and social improvement for women, they were undertaking important voluntary work. In 1924 the Egyptian Feminist Union established a school for the education of orphans and poor girls. They were to be taught to read and write and trained to earn their living by such means as sewing, embroidery and carpet weaving. Cultural and intellectual improvement was not forgotten. Thinkers and reformers were invited to speak on women's emancipation. A free day hospital was attached to the school.

Education, health and consciousness-raising were among the basic aims of most voluntary welfare work at the time. Women's associations, social, cultural or political, mushroomed in all parts of the country. Voluntary social work was a major item on all their agendas.

The period between 1919 and 1942 witnessed the establishment of a number of important voluntary associations. They have all flourished and are still continuing their good work.

Health Improvement Association

The Health Improvement Association started in a modest way through the efforts of six young women, led by Lily Daws. Now it has branches in nearly all parts of the country. It undertakes social, health and educational work on a large scale. Its basic aim is combating tuberculosis in cooperation with the Ministry of Health. It treats tuberculosis patients, looks after them during convalescence and finances small businesses for them when they fully recover. In this way, they can earn a living and support their families.

Daughter of an ex-Pasha ("Pasha" was the highest official title of honor under the monarchy), Lily Daws discovered the deplorable conditions in which tuberculosis patients lived and decided to do something about it, with the help of friends. They started to visit the chest diseases hospital. They talked to the patients, brought them food, then began to think of more hygienic housing for them. They started by renting modest premises and finally built a whole city in the Pyramids Desert in 1947.

Now the Association has a nursery and a primary and secondary school. There is also a technical school to educate and rehabilitate the children of the patients under its care. A textile mill produces hospital materials and is staffed by the technical school graduates. In addition there is a rehabilitation center, three family planning centers, a comprehensive treatment clinic and a center for anti-tuberculosis inoculation. The Association has come a long way since the time when Lily Daws was proud to drive a truck to carry equipment, in order to save funds. (Picture shows Lily Daws speaking at an HIA meeting.)

Other voluntary associations address their efforts to specific groups: children, women, the elderly, delinquent or handicapped. There are the Light and Hope Association which looks after blind girls and Loyalty and Hope Association for the rehabilitation of war heroes.

Candidates for parliament have gradually obtained more support from women voters. After a rather modest beginning, women now vote in greater numbers. Voting is obligatory for men but women are free to decide whether to vote or not. Gradually the number of women registered to vote has grown from 1% of the total number of voters in 1956 to 12% in 1972. It has increased substantially since.

Politics

First women in parliament With the 1952 Revolution's call for equality among all citizens, women acquired full political rights. In 1956 the new constitution granted women the right to vote and run for parliament on an equal footing with men. A number of women ran for election to the National Assembly (the only house of parliament at the time) in 1957. This attracted much notice and some controversy. But two candidates, Rawia Attia and Amina Shoukry, were elected and women were jubilant. The success of the pioneers encouraged other women to follow in their footsteps.

In the 1960 elections, six women won seats. Four years later the number increased to eight. Among them was the first Egyptian peasant woman to enter parliament: Fatma Diab. Two of these pioneers are still active in political life. Only three women were elected to the 1969 parliament. In 1971 the

Women voters on their way to the polls on election day. Women won their right to vote in 1956 and have since participated in increasing numbers as voters and parliamentarians.

National Assembly was re-named the People's Assembly and nine women were elected.

Parliamentary seats reserved for women The year 1979 witnessed significant changes in the area of women's participation in parliament. According to a 1979 law, 30 seats were to be reserved for women, one at least for each governorate (the country is divided into 26 governorates, each headed by a governor). In addition women were free to contest other seats. Over 200 women ran for the 30 reserved seats. Three women ran against men and won. Two more women were appointed by the President. The number of women in parliament was for the first time 35 out of 390. In 1985 the reserved seats were abolished as women were thought capable of fending for themselves.

Women in the Consultative Assembly In 1979 too, through an amendment in the constitution, a second house of parliament was created: the Consultative Assembly. Out of its 210 members, two-thirds were to be elected and one-third appointed by the President.

In the 1980 elections, two women were elected and five appointed. No seats were reserved for women. By then, there were 42 women in the Egyptian parliament.

Rawia Attia speaking in parliament. She is one of the first two women to be elected to the National Assembly, in 1957.

In parliament, women sit on various committees. Important committees such as those for culture, foreign affairs, legislation and housing have been chaired by women at various times. Women are playing a more significant role in decision-making regarding national issues. They often help with local needs too.

Who are the women in parliament?
Women in parliament are drawn from nearly all sections of society. They come in almost equal numbers from urban and rural areas. The majority are women with a university education. One of the first two women to serve in the National Assembly, Rawia Attia, was an ex-teacher who became a journalist. The other, Amina Shoukry, was involved in welfare work.

Women who serve in parliament are generally successful career women with a record of professional experience. Many have participated in some kind of voluntary social work or women's consciousness-raising projects. Most but not all had some party connection.

The '60s also witnessed women gaining access to another male preserve, diplomacy. Two young women, Abeyya el-Nafarawi and Hoda el-Marassi, were respectively appointed the first woman attaché at the Egyptian embassy in London and the first diplomat in the Paris embassy. Several women were then named cultural attachés and consuls. Finally in 1979 Dr. Aisha Rateb was appointed Egypt's first woman ambassador.

Women in government Until fairly recently, women in senior positions in government were the exception. Women mainly filled the rank and file of government departments as typists, clerks and secretaries. However, attitudes about women's work have been changing and women have been pushing forward to more effective roles in this area. Not only have women realized their own worth, but with better training and proven efficiency, they have been gradually moving on to managerial positions ranging from deputy-director and under-secretary to senior under-secretary (an under-secretary is immediately subordinate to the minister). In the early 1960s, a woman under-secretary was a novelty in Egypt. Since then, there have been several under-secretaries in the various ministries. It is true that women are still under-represented in top levels, but improvement is occurring.

First Egyptian women ministers In 1962 Dr. Hekmat Abu Zeid, university professor of sociology, was appointed Minister of Social Affairs. She remained in office for three years. In 1971 Dr. Aisha Rateb, professor of international law, filled the same ministerial post. Since 1977 Dr. Amal Othman, another law professor, has been Minister of Social Affairs and Insurance. Egypt looks forward to having more than one woman minister and the first governor. However, it can be safely claimed that with women in parliament and government, policy making no longer resides with men alone.

Business

Women have always been involved in business. Peasant women took the products of the field to market. Others sold homemade butter and cheese. These were mainly women of the less privileged class. At one point, business was regarded as inappropriate for middle-class women. In the last few decades even women of the upper class have ventured into the business world. To do so, women generally must possess initiative, self-confidence and the courage to take risks.

Women figure prominently in banking, insurance, accounting, and large companies. They serve not only as typists and secretaries but as insurance agents, bank assistant managers, and heads of departments. They have become legal accountants, tax officials, and currency experts.

In big business Most of the business activities in Egypt have been associated with the service sector and to some extent with construction and industry. Women have been successful in the areas of advertising, public relations, tourism, and import and export.

A few have made large investments especially in ready-made clothes for both the local market as well as the export market. One of the two best makes of women's knitwear is produced and marketed by a woman, Abdine. A number of women have excelled in creating exclusive ladies' wear. Their fashion shows attract the cream of society. They cater to working women, producing simple but smart clothes for them. Two of these designers, Laila al-Bannan and Madame Aziz, occasionally hold fashion shows for welfare aims, organized by the YWCA (Young Women's Christian Association) of Egypt.

There has been at least one large construction company run by a woman. Women have also ventured into the field of agriculture, particularly in the newly reclaimed desert areas. This is, however, a field for the adventurous, whether men or women.

Sufan Sufwan, general manager of the Foreign Operations Division, Egyptian Saudi Finance Bank. Banking is one field of business which attracts many women.

Mervet Masoud, owner of an art gallery (*above*) and tourist guide (*opposite*). Many women have ventured into small businesses such as running an art gallery or being tourist guides.

Women in multinational enterprises There are not many women in multinational enterprises, but those who ventured into this area are very successful. The representatives in Egypt of such major enterprises as General Motors, ALCOA and Nestlé are women. The open-door policy initiated by President Sadat in the early '70s has encouraged greater investments in various business areas. Some cinema actresses invest in the film industry.

Small- and medium-size business Apart from the few big investors, most women in business prefer small- or medium-size enterprises. Some women prefer what may be called a one-woman show, with one or two assistants if need be.

To combine business with a love of art, some women have opened small art galleries in their homes. Artists, particularly painters, pay for the use of the place in addition to a commission on sales. This is a rather classy kind of business, mostly undertaken by cultured women with means and beautiful houses with sufficiently large rooms for galleries.

Tourism is another area which women find attractive and profitable, mainly as tourist guides. Women with a knowledge of one or two foreign languages have the first prerequisite for the job. An advantage of this kind of business is that it is a one-woman enterprise.

Another kind of business run by women is the state-sponsored small family business. The Ministry of Social Affairs provides loans for the purchase of materials and equipment, and markets the products. The profits go to the producers. This project aims essentially at training housewives to earn some money to increase family income. The women make garments including knitwear, embroidered linen and underwear and street clothes, as well as rugs, brass and wood handicrafts and low-priced furniture.

The food business

The food business is becoming a popular kind of small business with women who do not want to work outside their homes. They mostly have no professional training but they love cooking. They produce made-to-order confectioneries, cakes, cookies, pastries, or the entire menu for special occasions such as birthdays, anniversaries and small parties.

This kind of service is particularly welcomed by working women who have little time for elaborate cooking. It is a profitable small business that needs neither a large budget nor advertising. The venture usually begins in a small way to help friends. Then the good news spreads and there is a rush of customers.

Women's magazines for sale. Women have always used the print media to voice their opinions.

Mass Media

Women in the press Women's contribution to the Egyptian press dates from 1892, when the first women's paper, *The Young Woman*, was published by a woman. It aimed at defending women's causes and encouraging women to take an interest in social issues.

With the beginning of the 20th century and the increasing clamor for women's emancipation, women's magazines flourished. The first half of the century witnessed the appearance of numerous journals issued mainly by women. Their titles reveal the varied viewpoints on women's roles and status in society: *Women's Renaissance, Hope, Mother of the Future* and *The Egyptian Woman*. Women's rights were a common topic. The importance of women's education was emphasized.

Militant magazines insisted that women must struggle for their rights.

The Egyptian Woman Hoda Shaarawi published two magazines carrying the same title, *The Egyptian Woman*. The first, in French (1925–1940), was addressed to the outside world. The second, in Arabic (1937–1940), explained the policy of the Egyptian Feminist Union.

In the editorial of the first Arabic issue Hoda Shaarawi addressed leading men in all areas of public life—thinkers, reformers, politicians, economists, educationists—as well as the ordinary man in the street, in an attempt to rally their support. When she turned to women, she specifically addressed women in their homes, in the factory, the field, the housewife in her palace or cottage, and the working mother. The contributors to this issue were eminent women and men, including nationalist leader, Mustafa Kamel, the prominent journalist Fikri Abaza and the writer Tawfiq al-Hakim.

Rose al-Youssef Rose al-Youssef's weekly, the *Rose al-Youssef*, has had the longest life span of all women's magazines: It was begun in 1925 and is still in publication today. It is a social and political magazine which supports women's struggle. Rose al-Youssef, a fearless journalist, sponsored women's right to work in journalism. Women have found the best opportunities for work in the magazine as authors of editorials and reporters covering social, political and other issues.

Present-day women journalists

Women journalists are no longer restricted to women's issues. They specialize in nearly all areas of life. However, some aspects of women's lives such as their dual roles in society, family laws and discrimination where it exists still form some of their major preoccupations.

Women are more visibly and dynamically involved in the press than ever before. They occupy all ranks in the field. They serve as editors, heads of departments, columnists, and reporters. They have reached the top position of chief editor, beginning with Amina al-Said, the militant pioneer, who occupied the post for *Hawa* for many years.

Following in her footsteps, women journalists have proved their worth. Not only are there several chief editors of both women's and general magazines, but some women columnists are among the press elite. *Al-Ahram* (*The Pyramid*), the most widely-read national paper, for example, boasts of such top women journalists as Amal Bakeir, Sana el-Beissi and Baheira Mokhtar. Scores of other brave and capable women play significant roles in many other papers and magazines.

Popular television personality, Nelly, introducing a television quiz program, *El-Fwazeer*. Women are involved in television and radio not only as actresses and presenters, but also as producers, directors, scriptwriters and heads of departments.

Women in television and radio
Women play a vital role in both television and radio. Anyone watching Egyptian television or listening to an Egyptian radio broadcast will discover their prominent role. Since the beginning of radio broadcasting in 1934 and that of television in 1960, women have been visibly active in these areas.

As part of the Ministry of Information, radio and television pursue the state policy of equal opportunity for both sexes. Job vacancies are widely advertised and recruitment for all jobs as well as training courses for promotion are open to men and women alike. Selection is generally open and competitive and so is promotion. Women have every opportunity of excelling and reaching top positions.

Both the radio and television stations have been repeatedly run by women. Television has had three women chief executives since its beginning: Tomader Tawfiq, Safeyya al-Mohandis and Samia Sadeq. Moreover, women occupy 70% of managerial posts. Certainly women have a large say in decision making and the policy in this vital medium.

Generally, women in Egyptian television do not suffer from job segregation. However, there are more women in wardrobe and make-up and more men in set building and painting.

But in the vital production area, women make up a large proportion. They are employed not only in junior grades as production assistants and continuity announcers, but as producers, directors and scriptwriters. Thirty percent of directors and scriptwriters are women. Of the work force in production, 50% are women. Their increasing participation in this area, once largely a male preserve, is encouraging.

The two main channels of Egyptian television are directed by women. Other women occupy key positions as directors of production, educational programs, announcers' department, and the Radio and Television Institute, which trains personnel.

Besides regular women's and children's programs, women are involved in preparing and presenting important programs in the areas of music, arts, tourism, science and literature as well as programs which deal with everyday problems like rising prices and housing problems. Among the popular programs made by women are *On the Road*, *Adam and Eve*, *Round the Galleries* and *Camera Round*. Owing to women's predominance in television, it is one workplace which provides women with child care facilities.

Literature

In pre-Islamic times, the Arabic poem always started with lines of *ghazal* ("praise of women"). Since then the traditional poetic image of the woman as a love object has greatly changed. Inspired by women's demonstrations for national independence in 1919, for example, Hafiz Ibrahim, the People's Poet (a title awarded to distinguished poets), wrote a poem to celebrate their courage. Tawfiq al-Hakim (1898–1987), a leading dramatist, who for some time was described as an enemy of women, created several significant female characters in his plays, *Isis*, *Pygmalion* and *The Tree Climber*.

Women and compassionate novelists

In the novel, women characters generally play more varied roles. They reflect changing patterns of national lifestyles. The first Egyptian novel *Zainab* (1914) by Mohamad Hassanain Haikal significantly has a woman's name for the title. It tells the story of a poor peasant girl who cannot marry the man she loves and dies of a broken heart. The novelist condemns the traditions which ignore personal choice and calls for individual freedom, especially for women. Both Taha Hussain in *The Call of the Curlew* (1941) and Youssef Idris in *The Sin* (1977) express great compassion for women's suffering.

In his great *Trilogy* published in the '50s, Naguib Mahfouz, winner of the Nobel Prize for Literature, paints a rich gallery of women: dedicated wives and mothers, inaccessible sweethearts, dancer-singers, prostitutes, and women at the crossroads between the old and the new.

The *Trilogy* traces the life story of a middle-class family living in Gammaliya, one of the older Cairo districts, during the period between the two world wars. The process of change in women's position is clearly reflected in its three volumes. The wife in the first volume, though the family cornerstone, is almost a prisoner of the home. The second generation daughters are slightly less confined. It is only the third-generation wife of a grandson that has an education and a job—a novelty, but gradually accepted.

In Mahfouz's later novels, as in those of younger writers, the traditional stereotypes give way to more emancipated and forceful female images. This is particularly true of the novelists of the last three decades, such as Mohamad al-Qaaid and Maguid Tobiya.

Women novelists The novel gives the writer greater scope for showing how social and political conditions affect a person's life. In Egypt, as elsewhere, there are more women novelists than dramatists.

In a largely autobiographical novel, *The Open Door* (1960), Latifa al-Zayyat writes about the formative years of a young girl growing up in a conservative family. Laila is intelligent and ambitious. She wants to live her own life and make the most of it. It is difficult but she succeeds. The novel is rich in human experience on both the personal and national levels. It is an exceptionally mature novel for its time. Says Latifa, "I recreated the history of the national movement from 1946 to 1956, implying the need for further change....The novel...is a dramatic narrative bearing the seeds of change for the characters and signifying more change on the national level."

Later women novelists moved from writing romantic dream novels to search-for-identity and self-fulfillment-type novels. Among the more established names are Zainab Sadeq, Iqbal Baraka, Fawzia Mahran and Sakina Fouad. Radwa Ashour represents a later generation.

In *Don't Steal the Dreams* (1978), Zainab Sadeq writes about the changes which occurred in the '70s and '80s, regarding personal relationships and women's role in public life. She reveals her preoccupation with how difficult it is for women to fulfill their dreams.

In *The Night Fatma was Arrested: Taming Man* (1980), Sakina Fouad writes about a brave woman who stands for what is right even when corruption is too strong to defeat. In vain she fights to save her errant brother. Adapted for television, the novel achieved great success.

In portraying a well-to-do family, Radwa Ashour creates two memorable women characters in her novel *Khadiga and Sawsan*: the wife and mother, clever but dictatorial, and her rebellious daughter. Khadiga manages not only her husband's hospital but her children's lives—except Sawsan's. Sawsan is involved in a painful struggle but she finally leads an independent life. She is

Women writers were at first mainly concerned with women's liberation. Later the feminist activist tone was somewhat subdued and more complex human issues were treated. Themes of love and marriage and the conflict between inherited traditions and personal choice persisted. But both the vision and treatment considerably varied and matured.

the only one whom the father entrusts with the secret of his having another wife. In this novel, Radwa ably explores women's psychological and social struggles against the frustrating social and historical forces.

Iqbal Baraka wrote six novels between 1971 and 1985. Three of her novels have been made into films and one serialized for television. Explaining how she came to write her novels, she says, "I realized from the beginning the importance of economic independence, complete self-reliance and a sense of responsibility. My heroines share these qualities with me. The pivotal theme in my novels is: 'What is freedom?' Most of my heroines are emancipated but they pause halfway, uncertain whether to go forward or to retreat. Often their final decisive resolution is to go ahead."

Fawzia Mahran, novelist.

Women dramatists

Egyptian women have written plays since the 1950s. Sophie Abdalla is a pioneer. More recently, in the early '80s, Fathiyya el-Assal wrote *Without Masks* in defense of women. Like similar problem plays, it was rather didactic.

A step forward was achieved by the late Nehad Gad in two plays dealing with more complex women's issues. *Adila: A Monodrama* deals with the everyday problems, dreams and disappointments of an ordinary housewife married to an unambitious husband.

The Bus Stop presents a wife who goes to work in an oil country, bringing back money and household appliances, only to find a tragic surprise waiting for her. Her husband has divorced her and remarried without her knowledge. She has nowhere to go.

Above: Well-known painter Gazibiyya Sirri at work.

Opposite: A tapestry workshop at the Wissa Wassef art school. Here students are taught the traditional craft of weaving and are encouraged to use their imagination and skills to create works of art.

Women painters

Beginning in 1923, women were sent abroad to study art. Later they joined art institutes and colleges at home. As time went on, women painters, like the men, exhibited their work either individually or in groups. They also participate in the annual exhibitions organized by the Ministry of Culture. Some accomplished painters have held exhibitions abroad and won international awards. Their numbers have been increasing in the last few decades. Among the best known are Margaret Nakhla, Khadiga Riyad, Tahiyya Halim, Inji Aflatoun and Gazibiyya Sirri.

Women art patrons Well-to-do women encouraged art exhibitions. In 1919 when graduates of the School of Fine Arts thought of holding an exhibition, a group of women formed a committee to organize the Spring Exhibition. They not only purchased some of the work for themselves, but in the name of the Egyptian Women's Committee bought others to decorate ministry offices.

Crafts

Apart from excelling in the areas of jewelry-making, ceramics and glass works, women have shown great talent in weaving tapestries. Two experiments

Inji Aflatoun

Inji Aflatoun (1924–1989) is one of the most renowned Egyptian women artists. She was poet, painter and determined feminist activist. As a painter, she has been described as "The Lady of Optimistic Colors." She drew trees, faces, the pain and misery of women whose lives have gone bad, high fences. But above all, she loved joyous colors and the movement of bodies meeting nature. Her paintings have been described as a song to life and communal work such as harvesting and picking cotton.

Although the daughter of a rich family, she loved the simple people of Egypt. She left the palatial family home to paint the mud houses, peasants and animals. Just as she loved the small villages and the fields, she was deeply moved by desert life.

She liked painting peasant women at harvest times and strove to catch the quick movements of their bodies and hands as they gathered the crop.

to turn weaving tapestries into a creative art have been in progress in the last few decades in Egypt. The first is in Harraniya, not far from the Giza Pyramids. The second flourishes in Akhmim, a small old town in Upper Egypt.

The Harraniya experiment Both experiments stem from a recognition of the latent gifts possessed by peasant children and a desire to encourage them to use them. The Harraniya experiment was started by Ramses Wissa Wassef, an architect and art teacher. Boys and girls from local peasant families are taught the simple craft of weaving, then encouraged to use their imagination to spontaneously create tapestries of great beauty. They do not work according to a plan or design. They freely create scenes from the environment. They gradually produce ingenious artistic creations, immensely valued worldwide. Throughout, Wassef was assisted by his wife, Sophie. After his death, his two daughters have continued the good work.

Concert pianist Mushira Eissa is internationally known.

The Akhmim art and life center Unlike the Harraniya center, this is part of a larger community development enterprise of the Christian Association of Upper Egypt. It aims at the education and development of deprived women. One of the means adopted to achieve this aim is the revival of authentic old weaving traditions for which Akhmim has long been famous.

The center is run by a small team of women. It is open to girls and women 15 years and older. It offers them the chance to develop their gifts through weaving and embroidery either through spontaneous artistic creations or the reproduction of ancient weaving motifs, particularly from Coptic textiles. Tapestries produce scenes from daily life: market day, harvesting, baking. They abound with men, women, children, animals, birds, trees, the Nile, houses, churches, and mosques. The center encourages free expression and an atmosphere of creativity. The women in the center find in art a means of self-fulfillment and a way to freedom.

Music
Egyptians love music and singing. Women excel in these areas. The greatest Egyptian singer is Om-Kolthoum (she is profiled in chapter 5). Other singers like Shadia, Nagat and Suzan Atiyya draw large audiences and sing on radio and television. Their tapes are best-sellers. Faida Kamel is well known as a singer of national songs.

Women musicians have been important members of the Cairo Symphony Orchestra since its establishment in the '50s. Egypt has also lately produced two internationally-famous women pianists: Marcelle Matta and Mushira Eissa.

On stage and screen
It was in 1915 that the first woman appeared on the Egyptian stage. However, until the Higher Institute for Dramatic Arts was established in 1944, there were few professionally-trained actresses. Since then, both the stage and cinema have been attracting women combining talent and training. Besides the renowned pioneer, Amina Rizq,

Faten Hamama, the child actress who went on to act in movies which dealt with the changing status of women and working women's problems.

there are such leading actresses as Samiha Ayyoub, Thana Gamil, Suad Hosni, and Fardos Abdel-Hamid.

Faten Hamama: A rare talent Starting as a child actress, Faten Hamama went on to create a brilliant career for herself. From acting Cinderella roles, she went on to serious social dramas. She played characters that reflect social issues, particularly the changing status of women and working women's problems. She shone in the central characters of two literary classics: Taha Hussain's *Call of the Curlew* and Youssef Idris's *The Sin*.

Dance

A folkloric cabaret. Folkloric dance has been taken out of the village and developed into an art form for the stage.

A new opportunity for women to express themselves in dance was presented when folkloric dance troupes were organized—the first in 1959. Before, there were small local troupes which danced at festivals, but the new folkloric dance troupes are big professional troupes which stage nationwide performances.

The Reda folkloric dance troupe was founded in 1959. It largely owes its success to two gifted and dedicated artists, Mahmoud Reda and Farida Fahmi. Mahmoud, the artistic director and principal male dancer, researched and choreographed the dances. Farida, the inspired and talented female star of the troupe, helped Mahmoud to develop and gain nationwide recognition for this new dance form. The troupe began with 15 dancers, more than half of whom were women, and now has 150 dancers, musicians, and technicians.

Following the success of the Reda troupe, a national troupe was founded in 1960. Applicants to join were many, but only 46 were chosen. They gave their first performance in 1963 on the occasion of the 1952 Revolution celebrations.

Despite distinctive styles, both these troupes and several provincial ones dance to themes based on the customs and traditions of people in various parts of Egypt. The dances were set to the music of traditional instruments and choreographed according to modern techniques. The costumes are stylized, yet retained the local color. Among the dances are the stick, Bedouin, Nubian, candelabra, Girls of Alexandria and peasant wedding dances.

Sport

Physical training This has long been part of the educational program for girls. In 1937 an institute for physical training for girls was established to train physical education teachers. It was attached to one of the best girls' secondary schools. In 1947 a Higher Institute for Physical Training was founded. In the early '50s it was moved to better quarters, thanks to the efforts of Nefissa el-Ghamrawi, a pioneering sportswoman. She was appointed dean of the institute and retained this position for 22 years.

Sports for women In recent years, women have been increasingly attracted to sports. Girls practice sports at school. A few do so at college. They participate in athletic events and festivals. Popular sports include swimming, gymnastics, athletics, table-tennis, basketball, and volleyball. Other games like tennis, squash, croquet, golf and riding also attract women. Some girls have even tried karate. Most women, however, find little time for sports. With marriage and children, often on top of a job, regular participation in sporting activities is a Herculean undertaking.

Rare sportswoman

Nefissa el-Ghamrawi is the first Egyptian woman to study, plan and teach physical education to girls in Egypt. She also started the girl guides movement. Under her leadership, girls participated in numerous sporting events and festivals both in Egypt and abroad.

She is the first Egyptian to create a folkloric troupe for television. She started long distance swimming for women and was the first to practice this sport. She excelled in athletics, hockey and basketball.

A good year In 1991 Egyptian girls did their country proud in two important events held in Cairo: the Mediterranean Sports Competition and the All-Africa Games. In the former, competing with participants from Switzerland, France, Italy and San Marino, Egyptian girls won the first prize for water ballet. In the latter, they earned two gold medals in athletics and nine gold and 11 silver medals in swimming.

Water ballet is a sport in which Egyptian sportswomen excel.

Being Woman

T hough traditionally regarded as the weaker sex, women possess considerable innate strength. Though often viewed as seducer, they are entrusted with the rearing of children, the men and women of future generations. Because of this mixed attitude toward women, their role in society was often restricted, their freedom curtailed and their contribution to society undervalued.

Except in very few matriarchal societies, where women ruled, men have been regarded, and acted, as the undisputed head of the family. Women occupied a subservient position. This traditional arrangement of things still prevails in Egypt, particularly in rural and some poorer urban areas. Elsewhere, as a result of the spread of education in general and women's education and employment in particular, women in a large sector of society are gradually being seen less as subordinate and more as equal to men.

In the rural areas (*opposite*), women are still subservient to men, but women in the cities (*right*), particularly educated women, are gradually seen as equals to men.

In the home

An ordinary housewife is almost fully in charge of the household. She looks after the family, manages the home chores, either single-handedly or, if lucky, with some help. Most importantly, she often has charge of the budget. The woman has it in her power to reduce expenditure, cut down consumption and so reduce prices. She often has to do the shopping besides preparing the meals.

One woman supervising her children's homework (*right*), while another works as a desk clerk in a hotel (*opposite*). Married women are increasingly working outside the home.

An extra job for her is to tutor the children if they are of school age, and now and then help them with their homework. She cares for all members of the family, nursing them when they fall ill. These are some of her responsibilities, and she is mostly happy with them.

The husband as the breadwinner has some privileges. Husbands are mostly unwilling to help around the house or look after small babies. However, this is slowly changing, especially with young husbands whose wives are working. In a recent television interview with young men, three out of four stated that they think it is only fair to assist their wives and share the household responsibilities with them.

The more traditional husbands like to take charge of the finances of the family, have some say in how the household should be run and have their wishes more or less regarded as commands. This is often the pattern when the wife does not have a job, and less often if she has one.

Varying degrees of constraints

Traditional constraints are stronger in some sections of society than in others, depending on various social and cultural as well as economic factors. On the whole, it is true to say that women today enjoy greater freedom than ever before. At one time, it was said that a young woman was governed first by her father, then by her husband or her brother. Now an educated woman has much more say in what she wants to do with her life. She is no longer bound by the will of her menfolk. A woman chooses her own career and, except very rarely, her own husband. She is more financially independent. She drives her own car and can travel alone.

One constraint still exists. It is still unacceptable for an unmarried young woman to live on her own, except in case of necessity, as when a young woman has a job away from where her family lives. This mostly occurs in the case of teachers and doctors newly appointed to government posts in different parts of the country. Living quarters are often provided in the workplace.

Married working women

Married women are increasingly working outside the home. They mostly start working after graduating from college or after obtaining some kind of vocational training at a technical or commercial institute. After marriage, they generally retain their jobs. Some prefer to stay at home when they have children, and maybe go back to work when the children go to school. Some men prefer their wives not to work. It is a young woman's privilege to accept a marriage proposal or reject it if the terms do not suit her.

Modern home appliances have considerably reduced the time and energy needed for home chores. The most serious problem for a working woman is child care in the preschool years. Day care centers and nurseries are widely established by the Ministry of Social Affairs, private sector and religious organizations.

Women workers in a garment factory. The state is concerned with the pressures on working women who have to take on diverse roles and has sought to ease their burdens through various measures.

State concern for working women's dual roles

The woman is viewed by the state as a human being, as a person responsible for her family and finally as contributing to the social and economic development of society. There is therefore a deep concern to ease the pressures of her diverse roles, through legislative and other measures.

A study conducted on a sample of working women from all classes revealed that about one-third of the women surveyed had no problems. The rest basically suffered, in decreasing degrees, from transportation and child care problems and difficulty of coordinating working hours with personal obligations. Some women work for organizations that provide transportation. Legislation aims at coping with other difficulties.

But some measures stipulated by law

Legislative measures to assist working women

The employment law of 1959 stipulates:

- The right of a working woman to her end-of-service remuneration or pension fund entitlement, should she resign to marry or to have a baby.
- A woman cannot be dismissed if she does not report to work because of illness resulting from pregnancy or delivery.
- A mother is entitled to nurse her baby twice during working hours without any decrease in her salary.
- The employer should provide day care facilities if 100 or more women are employed in the same workplace.

Article 11 of the 1971 constitution stipulates that the government co-ordinates a woman's duties toward her family with her work for society, and holds the government responsible for the protection of mothers and children.

According to the Labor Law of Civilian Workers and the Public Sector Law of 1978, working mothers enjoy a number of privileges, such as:

- The right to a three-month delivery leave with full pay, three times during her term of employment.
- If so authorized by the authorities concerned, the right to work half-time on half salary.
- The right to maternity leave without pay to look after a child for a maximum period of two years each time, three times throughout her term of employment.
- The right to a leave without pay to accompany her husband who is authorized to go abroad.

are not always implemented. For example, the law enforcing the opening of a nursery in a workplace having 100 women workers and above is often evaded by means of employing fewer than 100 women in the same place or by providing unsatisfactory facilities. As in other countries, the willingness or refusal to recognize family responsibilities in the workplace is a very real issue for women, as they, the women, are mainly responsible for them.

Shopping at the government-run store. The government's social welfare program for women includes the provision of goods and services for busy working women at cooperatives and other government-run agencies.

Leave to look after a child Quite a few working mothers who have babies take advantage of this kind of leave. For, although this is unpaid leave, the pension fund contribution, amounting to about one-third of the salary, is paid by the employer. In addition, the working mother resumes her job at the end of the leave without much loss.

An hour off to nurse the baby This is another popular measure stipulated by law. Often, instead of having two half-hour breaks during a working day, this is altered to going to work an hour later or leaving work an hour earlier than scheduled time—a more practical arrangement especially if the mother lives at some distance from the workplace.

Women's social welfare program

Since Egypt signed the agreement concerning the elimination of all forms of social discrimination against women adopted by the United Nations at the International Women's Decade Conference in Copenhagen in 1980, several important developments occurred in women's programs in Egypt. A number of associations were established and projects drawn up to secure women's rights.

A general department for women's affairs was established within the Ministry of Social Affairs to look after women's concerns as wife, mother and working women.

A National Committee for Women was set up by the Ministry of Social Affairs to plan programs for women's advancement and coordinate projects initiated by different ministries concerning women's rights, social, legal and political.

The Working Women's Centers Project is implemented by the Ministry of Social Affairs to provide working women with some services such as ready-to-cook meals at cooperatives, ready-made clothes and domestic service at a fixed daily rate.

Family guidance and advisory bureaus were established by the Ministry of Social Affairs in various towns and villages to help resolve family problems.

Social security and social assistance for working women and their families were established.

The National Council for Childhood and Motherhood, set up in 1988, draws up the strategy for childhood and motherhood in Egypt. It proposes programs and coordinates their implementation among the different ministries.

A project for guidance of women was launched to make women aware of their duties and rights as stipulated by the various acts, laws and decrees. Other aims of the project were to acquaint women with the procedures to be followed when applying for service to a public department, and to give information about the service bureaus attached to ministries and government bodies to which women could go for assistance. To achieve these aims, regular meetings for women were held at community centers and pamphlets were published. House visits were also made.

Women's work force complaints

Despite the great efforts exerted to assist working women, complaints about the difficulties of coordinating their dual roles are occasionally voiced. In her weekly column in the national newspaper, *Al-Ahram*, Magda Mehanna claims that the problem is not the result of lack of professional efficiency on the woman's part, but a general unwillingness to seriously discuss the problems confronting working women, to admit their size and attempt to solve them.

Why does a woman work?

There are several reasons why a woman works. For some women, it is because of a desire for economic independence. Sometimes women are driven by necessity to work, as rising costs of living mean that one income in the family is not nearly enough. There are yet some women who work because of a love of work or because they want to fill in their time. Nearly all women who work contribute their whole income or part of it to the family budget. Women continue to work also because work satisfies a need and enhances their self-esteem.

Women's performance in the work force

Investigations have shown that the working woman is less productive than

A fruit seller (*right*) and women workers in a government office (*opposite*). For some women, it is necessary to work in order to supplement the family income. For others work satisfies a desire for economic independence or a need for self-fulfillment.

the man. Her low productivity is due to repeated absence or late arrival at the workplace as a result of family problems. This applies to married women with children.

However, women in industry are less liable to injury than men and are more cautious and accurate in using machinery. Working women are less likely to break the rules. In managerial posts, they are more positive in decision making.

Workers' unions and professional syndicates

Having set foot in public life and most areas of work, women sought to become members of professional syndicates and workers' unions. They have also served on the boards of directors of several professional syndicates. Fatma Enan was deputy chairman of the teachers' syndicate for several years. She came to be called the "The Teachers' Mother." There are more women in the syndicates representing professions where women are active in larger numbers, such as those of journalists, teachers, the medical profession, dentists, and lawyers. There are fewer women in the syndicates representing engineers and agriculturists. Women workers, like men workers, are unionized, and there are some women union leaders, one of the earliest being Aida Fahmi.

Women's conferences

Egyptian women have participated in conferences held to discuss women's problems in general and working women in particular. In the last few decades, several such conferences were held in Cairo. Two of them concentrated on women's role in administration and the most suitable means to train women for leadership.

Egyptian women have also participated in Arab, regional and international conferences, notably the Women's Decade conferences in Copenhagen in 1980 and Nairobi in 1985.

A return to the veil?

In the last two decades, some women, generally referred to as "veiled women" have been adopting Islamic dress. This is partly due to fundamentalist influence. Islamic dress consists of an ankle length outfit with long sleeves and a head cover that covers the head and neck, sometimes surrounding the face. In some versions, the face is covered except for two slits for the eyes.

In most cases there is no appreciable difference between the "veiled" women and other women. They go to college and mix with their male colleagues. Despite repeated calls for women to stay at home in some circles, they continue to work. Some are even active in public life.

This call for women to stay home and the wearing of Islamic dress have their proponents and opponents. Activist feminists are strongly opposed to both. Feminists oppose the veil because they feel it is associated with sex segregation.

Women and religion

Moslem and Christian women are brought up more or less the same way. They go to the same schools and work side by side. Naturally their forms of worship are different. One thing, however, they share. Voluntary charity service is one of their most cherished goals. Many churches and mosques have women's committees deeply involved in welfare work. Furthermore, various religious associations formed by women are active in organizing and implementing programs for women, children, the elderly and for health services.

Among such organizations are the Islam Women's Association, Maadi Child Association and Moslem Women's Association as well as the Orthodox Church Women's Committee, the Federation of Protestant Women and Women Friends of the Bible Association.

The kind of services they render to women range from consciousness-raising and comprehensive development programs aimed at social, cultural and economic development to running hostels for young women away from home, nurseries for working women's children and homes for elderly women, besides various cultural and religious activities.

Opposite: Women leaving the Moslem Women's Association. Religious women's associations provide a wide range of services for women.

Rural women

About 57% of Egyptian women live in rural areas. In addition to their ordinary household chores and caring for the children, they are often expected to help in the fields. In the last three decades, many male agricultural workers have gone to the cities to take temporary jobs or to the oil countries on temporary migration to look for work. The women are left at home to care for the

family and cultivate the land. The rural woman has to shoulder more responsibilities than her urban sister, especially under the more traditional village lifestyle.

Illiteracy is highest in the rural areas. Despite the enormous efforts exerted in the areas of adult education, literacy classes and regular education, illiteracy is still a problem, especially for women.

Health, social, economic and consciousness-raising programs are undertaken to improve the standard of living of the rural inhabitants, uproot less desirable customs and traditions and promote better ways of life. Progress may be slow, but results are encouraging.

Overpopulation problems and village values One of the serious problems Egypt has to deal with is overpopulation. The population increases by about one and a quarter million annually. The rate of increase is highest in rural areas. For rural families, the more children, the better. Not only do children start early to contribute to the family income, but a large family is regarded as an asset as it is more economically productive. A rural woman, therefore, tends to have several children in quick succession. If she has only daughters, she will continue to try to have a son. Sometimes there is the worry that if she does not, her husband may be tempted to marry a second wife. This is not just a matter of preferring boys to girls, but is part of a deeply rooted tradition that a son bears the family name and keeps inheritance in the family.

Under certain conditions, such as lack of education, women bear the brunt of old values and traditions which perpetuate the population problem and hinder progress. Family planning programs are thus largely addressed to women, in the hope that they can also influence their husbands.

Consciousness-raising As radio and television reach the farthest parts of the country, several programs geared to comprehensive development are broadcast through these media. There are several radio and television programs that aim at women's consciousness-raising. They encourage rural women to participate in social and cultural programs, and to make use of available financial resources from the government, voluntary organizations and international bodies. They acquaint the rural woman with the measures necessary to increase family income. Such programs also aim at enhancing women's self-reliance by encouraging them to participate in decision making, planning, and implementing and evaluating development programs.

Rural women have responded positively to the programs organized for them, including literacy, family planning and health care classes.

Turning away from agriculture The number of women workers in agriculture has been decreasing. They are turning away from agriculture and taking up more profitable economic occupations. An important result of this is the dwindling of their traditional contribution to food production in such areas as poultry, eggs and milk products, particularly high-quality cheese.

There is a need to get rural women involved in mechanical agriculture and

rural food industries. The Ministry of Social Affairs is dealing with this through a rural women's development program. This program aims, among other things, to provide rural women with tools as well as the training to use them.

One project to promote the rural woman's contribution to the country is the women's leadership project. It aims at training female leaders to help urban and rural women solve their problems. In the villages, some women were chosen from different villages and trained to teach other rural women family planning, how best to bring up their children, increase the family economic resources, and eradicate illiteracy.

A women's club project and rural promotion project teach the village women crafts and provide loans for setting up a small cottage industry.

Baking bread with a traditional oven (*opposite*) and carrying water at the Fayyum Oasis (*above*). Women in rural areas live a more conservative and traditional lifestyle than their urban sisters. But even here life is changing as the broadcast media have reached the country and the government is making concerted efforts to develop the countryside.

The stick dance is one of the folk dances performed at weddings in the countryside.

market, apart from being a commercial enterprise, is also a social occasion for women. Harvesting, particularly cotton picking, is a festive time. Young men and women enjoy picking the large fluffs of cotton as they sing special joyous songs. The sale of the cotton produce is generally followed by numerous weddings.

Rural weddings Before the wedding, the bride's trousseau and household furniture are transported to the groom's home on horse-drawn carts in a procession headed by magnificently decorated dancing horses. Female relatives and friends follow, carrying presents. After passing through the village, the procession stops at the door of the groom's house and the household objects are carried into the house amid singing and dancing.

The night before the wedding two henna feasts are held, in the bride's and bridegroom's homes. "Henna" is a red dye traditionally used to color the hands and feet of the couple and their close friends and relatives as a sign of jubilation. Sometimes a troupe of singers and dancers is hired.

The bride's car is usually decorated with colorful ribbons. Ahead of it, some men perform the stick dance, a folk dance, or gather in a circle singing and dancing. Guns are fired in the air while women give joyful trills (*zaghrouda*).

Rural social and cultural traditions As the extended family is still the norm, household chores are shared by all the women in the family. Grandmothers help look after the children. An Egyptian proverb says, "The dearest children are the grandchildren." The mother-in-law is often a veritable matriarch, but just as often a source of comfort and assistance to the wife and mother.

Festive occasions Such occasions are frequent in village life. Going to the

Once a young man's proposal to marry a woman is accepted by her parents, he is required to present her with an engagement gift and a sum of money as a dowry, in addition to a wedding gown. The bride on her part has to provide the household furniture and kitchen utensils.

Women of Sinai

Sinai, a dear part of Egypt, has a rich history. As a center of Pharaonic civilization and the arena of epic struggles throughout the ages, its history is reflected in its inhabitants. Its historic roads witnessed the passing of the armies of Thutmose and Alexander the Great besides the prophet Abraham, Moses, the Holy Family, and the spread of Islam.

The people are mostly descendants of the Pharaohs in addition to some Bedouin tribes from the Arabian Peninsula. Bedouin qualities are dominant. The women's looks and characters are distinctive. They have a strong and persistent character and artistic gifts. Sinai women produce beautifully embroidered cotton galabias, loose garments worn by men and women, with magnificent cross-stitched designs. Their hand-woven *kelim* (rugs) are coveted possessions.

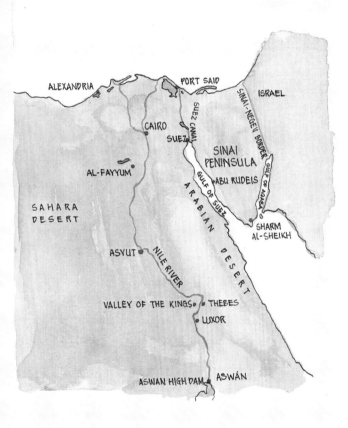

During the Israeli occupation in 1967–1979, the Sinai woman's true mettle was revealed. Amid great suffering, she continued the struggle for survival.

Sinai women strive to raise the cultural standards of their families. Their efforts have been so successful that the North Sinai Governorate has one of the highest rates of attendance in schools in the country, especially among girls. Not only have the women of Sinai pursued higher studies and taken up all kinds of jobs, but they also serve in parliament.

Women of the New Valley

Until fairly recently, old traditions prevailed in the New Valley in the heart of the Western Desert. Women were almost completely imprisoned at home. Older women could not go out except at night. Young women could only go out to have corn ground at the mill or to fill water jars. A bride's trousseau consisted of her clothes, a mattress and three clay water jars on a wooden stand.

A tremendous change has almost completely transformed the lifestyle in the Valley oases, Kharga, Dahkla and Farafra. The traditional image of the oases women wearing loose Bedouin clothes and tending a herd of sheep or goats has almost completely disappeared. Women now wear modern clothes, go to college, have jobs and serve in parliament. Women are predominant in the administrative posts of the police force and the local government office.

Women participate in literacy and family planning programs.

Oasis woman contractor

Ibtisam Abu-Rehab is an interesting example of a Kharga businesswoman. She started as a civil engineer in the housing department of the New Valley. Later she resigned and became a successful contractor. She became chairwoman of the New Valley Construction and Reconstruction Association. She fiercely competes for large construction projects and has won several of them.

Ibtisam is such a thorough contractor that she supervises the last touches of the huge buildings she constructs. She ably leads a team of 20 engineers and technicians and many workers. She still recalls how she started civil construction work while still a student at the Faculty of Engineering, and looks forward to fulfilling many more dreams.

Ibtisam Abu-Rehab was the first woman to drive a car in the New Valley. In resolutely challenging opposition, she established a driving school. Now many oasis women drive cars. She, however, prefers to drive a mini-truck.

chapter five

Profiles of Women

T he women in this chapter are all women who have played significant roles in society in Egypt in modern times. They are certainly not the only ones to have done so. Many others have left their mark on Egyptian society. These have been chosen as representatives of important women in various areas of social, political and professional life. They are particularly dynamic women, who have given generously of their time and energy to the service of society and the happiness of people either at home or in the world at large. They are all pioneers in vital areas of human life.

They come from different sectors of society, but they have served society as a whole. They have succeeded in achieving self-fulfillment, proving women's capability to succeed in areas previously closed to them, and setting an example for other women.

Young women of Egypt (*opposite and right*) who aspire to be more than somebody's daughter, wife or mother, are not short of role models, as there are women past and present who have led significant lives.

Rose al-Youssef

Rose al-Youssef ("ahl-YOO-sef") was a self-made woman who scaled the heights of success in more than one area. She started as an actress and excelled. Then she was drawn into the turbulent world of the press. She is mostly known as Rose al-Youssef, although after she married a Moslem, Mohamad Abdel-Qoddus, she adopted the name Fatma.

Rose al-Youssef, actress and publisher.

used to spend hours gazing at the stage, she wrote later, dreaming of one day wearing those strange clothes and being part of this world.

Sometimes she would find her way backstage. She would look with eagerness and curiosity at what was going on. She loved to imitate the way the actors talked and imitated their speeches. Her only wish was to be like them one day, repeating lines of poetry and uttering fiery words.

Luck smiles at little Rose One day a well-known actor, Omar Wasfy, saw her. He was a big man with large eyes and a loud voice. He was known for his terrifying looks. Under his gaze, she trembled and stuck to the wall. Unable to hide, she started crying.

Amid her tears, she saw another man come in. She recalls his appearance in her memoirs: "a short ugly man with a bent back...but his eyes were full of kindness and gentleness." He approached her, asking what was wrong. She did not answer, but stuck closer to the wall. He smiled, came closer and took her hand.

First steps to the stage This kind man turned out to be no less than the great theater actor and director Aziz Eid ("eed"). He took Rose to a small coffee house near the theater, offered her a soft drink and listened with interest to

As a little orphan Rose used to sneak into a theater in Cairo, the Dar al-Tamthiel al-Arabi (Arab Acting House), to see whatever play was on, eagerly watching what seemed to her the heroes and heroines of a strange, legendary world. She could hardly understand anything of the play, but was fascinated by what she saw: the lights, the colorful clothes, the characters, the action. She

her story. From then on, Aziz Eid was like a father to her.

Aziz used to say, "I cannot transform lead into gold, but I can discover gold and make it shine and glitter." And that was what he did in the case of Rose. With patience and gentleness, he trained the young girl. He treated her as an artist right from the start, watching for an opportunity to put her on the stage.

First enormous success Not long after taking Rose under his wing, Aziz was directing a play in which there was a character of an old woman. He could not persuade any of the young actresses to play the part. In a moment of inspiration, he thought of his young trainee and immediately started coaching her.

Rose's first appearance on stage was an enormous success. Her teacher was convinced she would be the best "tragedy" actress in Egypt.

Among the pioneers Rose al-Youssef's first steps along the hazardous path of success coincided with the beginnings of the Egyptian theater. For her as for others, there were ups and downs. But she was one of the pioneers. She worked with several of the great actors of the '20s and '30s, such as George Abyad and Naguib al-Rihani. She had a genuine talent for the theater. She played her best roles with the leading Ramses Troupe when Egyptian theater flourished in the early '20s.

One of the memorable roles she played was the challenging one of Marguerite Gautier in the well-known French play *La Dame aux Camélias*, in Arabic translation.

She continued to play leading female roles in several Arabic and translated foreign plays until she gave up acting in 1925 when she started a magazine. Nine years later, however, she made two more appearances. A small Egyptian village was tragically destroyed by fire. To help rebuild the village, she organized two charity performances for the benefit of the village. With some of her old colleagues, she presented a performance that dazzled and brought tears to large audiences.

Why not a magazine? Rose al-Youssef's initial steps in publishing did not entirely cut her off from the theater. When she cried once to some friends and colleagues, "Why not start an art magazine?" everyone thought this was a jest. However, she would not listen to any opposition, and decided on the spot to give the yet unborn magazine a name that she had used in the theater and which people loved, *Rose al-Youssef*. This was an even bigger joke, everyone said. But she was resolved. She had finally found her lifetime occupation.

The first issue of the *Rose al-Youssef* (*above*) was devoted to the development of art and literature in Egypt. Today, as a social and political magazine, it is an important medium for forming public opinion (*opposite*).

Rose al-Youssef In justifying her new enterprise, Rose al-Youssef wrote: "There was a great need for a respectable art magazine and for sound art criticism to [promote] the flourishing of art."

Preparations for *Rose al-Youssef* included working out a modest budget and gathering some keen pressmen. Among them was Mohamad el-Tabii, a brilliant theater critic, who later became assistant editor of the magazine. As all the money available did not exceed five pounds (about $12.50), hardly enough for paper and printing, everyone had to work for free in the beginning. Rose turned her home, a high-rise apartment, into temporary headquarters for *Rose al-Youssef*, declaring that anyone who wanted to work for the magazine had to climb 95 steps (leading to her apartment). Meanwhile, she went around to the government offices to get a license; officials were surprised to see a woman.

The first issue of the magazine appeared one morning in October 1925; Rose al-Youssef vowed to see it live and endure, and she did. She continued the struggle of pushing the magazine forward, despite all kinds of difficulties in a society where few women participated in intellectual activity.

Political involvement Not long after the appearance of the magazine, Rose published a daily paper under the same

The great difficulty of being a woman

"Invading the press arena," Rose al-Youssef wrote, "was a new and difficult enterprise for men, let alone women. In that climate, I had to proceed shouldering the responsibility of a work carrying my name, to launch attacks and be exposed to counter-attacks, chair an organization where all the workers were men, to go and meet ministers and high officials."

The difficulty, she said, was not the lack of money, the great effort needed or the limit of the market. "It was simply that I was a woman."

However, she was not to be discouraged or beaten. The magazine survived and endured. It attracted such eminent writers as Taha Hussain and Abbas al-Aqqad, and published national and world literature, and art subjects. Although originally conceived as an art magazine, *Rose al-Youssef* soon became an important medium for forming public opinion both culturally and politically.

name. She gradually became more involved in politics and national issues. During the political crisis between Egyptians and the British over independence, she supported Saad Zaghloul of the Wafd Party, whom she greatly admired. Wafd Party members started to read the magazine, first in secret because it was published by a woman, and later openly.

As she was a fearless critic of bad government, the magazine and the paper suffered. Biting criticism and satirical caricatures angered many politicians. Both works were repeatedly banned and the owner had to face persecution, bankruptcy and imprisonment.

Political changes meant a change of attitude toward Rose. Mustafa al-Nahhas, Zaghloul's successor, supported her at first. When an opposition party paper called the Wafd the "Rose al-Youssef Party," he retorted in a public speech saying that the Wafd was proud to be the Rose al-Youssef Party. When he withdrew his support, a violent demonstration occurred in front of the magazine offices. Undaunted, Rose confronted the angry crowd alone and spoke to the people who ended by cheering her.

A *true nationalist and journalist*

Through thick and thin, Rose remained true to her beliefs and principles, and to those who, in her opinion, stood bravely

for the national interest, condemning even those she had supported when they betrayed the people's trust. She remained head of her publishing business until it was handed over, flourishing, to her son in 1945. Ihsan Abdel-Qoddus has paid his mother a great tribute, saying proudly, "She made me the man I am."

In the words of Mustafa Amin, an important Egyptian journalist, she is "a woman with the courage of a thousand men."

Om-Kolthoum

Om-Kholthoum ("ohm-kol-THOOM"), born in 1904, grew up in a small village, Tomay al-Zahayra, which attained fame as the birthplace of Egypt's great singer. Her full name is Om-Kolthoum Ibrahim al-Biltagi, but she was always known by her first name. Her father, who was a reciter of the Koran and the life story of the prophet Mohammed, named her after the Prophet's daughter. She was five years old when she went to the village school, where she stayed for three years. At one point, she almost stopped going to school, because her father could not afford the small fee for both her and her brother. She learned reading and writing and some Koranic verses. She was said to be a naughty and clever child.

Early start Om-Kolthoum started her career as a singer quite early. She had a sweet voice and retentive memory. She used to listen to her father as he coached her brother in the reciting of the Koran and singing of religious songs, then sing to herself.

Her brother usually accompanied their father to village festivals and weddings where together they would recite the Koran and sing religious songs. One day her brother was ill, so Om-Kolthoum accompanied her father instead. She sang so beautifully that her fame soon spread. She sang in many villages. Her father was advised to take her to Cairo. After two short successful visits to Cairo, where she was greatly admired, she finally went to live there in 1923.

In Cairo she started to frequent musical gatherings, where she met composers and musicians and listened to their assessment of her singing. She was open to new ideas and respected the need to preserve the classical heritage side by side with modern melodies.

Scaling the heights of success Impressed by her accomplishments, the Institute of Oriental Music formed a new band, consisting of the best musicians, for her. Her records sold in great numbers. One favorite song had sales amounting to half a million records.

Her fame spread like wild fire with the beginning of Egyptian radio in 1934, and the opening of the first Egyptian film studio in 1936. The radio began broadcasting two Om-Kolthoum concerts per month from the radio station. Later concerts were broadcast from one of the theaters. These concerts came to be monthly events for people throughout the Arabic world, in homes, coffee houses and clubs.

Studio Misr, the first Egyptian film studio, opened with Om-Kolthoum's first film, a historical musical named *Wedad*. It was followed by five other films in which she played the part of a singer in some court or palace, in addition to a film based on the opera *Aïda*. She proved her competence both as singer and actress.

The poet and the singer Ahmad Rami, a young poet studying in Paris, heard that a brilliant young singer sang one of his poems. On his return home in 1924, Rami went to one of her concerts, was fascinated by her voice and asked her to sing his poem for him. That was the beginning of a long and fruitful relationship. The best of Rami's love

> Lines from Om-Kolthoum's songs have become part of the national heritage, expressing the wisdom of ages:
> "Aims are not achieved by wishes
> The world is conquered only through strife."
> "The whole world stood watching
> While I built the foundations of my glory alone
> When challenged, the pyramid-builders
> Spoke on my behalf."

poems were inspired by Om-Kolthoum. People came to think that while she sang his poems, a dialogue went on between the loving poet and his beloved.

In search of talent Aiming at perfection and innovation, Om-Kolthoum welcomed talented poets and musicians, young and old, to work with her. She was careful to address both the sophisticated and simple listeners. After a period of classical and romantic songs, she sang more realistic verse using simple vivid language, mainly during the '40s.

National songs Om-Kolthoum was a dedicated patriot. Her love for Egypt and her fellow citizens was expressed in passionate songs. She sang for Egypt, the Nile, freedom, and evacuation of foreign troops. Whether she sang calling for the struggle against the enemy, for promoting nationalist feeling or celebrating victory, she voiced the nationalist feelings of millions.

Touring the world for Egypt After Egypt's 1967 defeat in the Six-Day War with Israel, Om-Kolthoum spent all her energy in raising funds for the "war effort." She traveled all over the country and abroad, singing and collecting subscriptions, amounting to about $875,000. She sang in Kuwait, Morocco, Tunisia and Jordan. Her concert at the Olympia Theater in Paris was a great success, attended by Arabs and Europeans. After her return to Egypt, she received a letter from Charles De Gaulle, President of France at the time, saying, "Your voice touched my heart and the hearts of the French people."

Social welfare Om-Kolthoum was a generous woman, always ready to help without making a show of it. Some time before her death she started a welfare venture, "A Thousand Machines." At first she bought 400 sewing machines, but eventually obtained a total of 1,200. The aim was to provide young women evacuees from the Suez Canal Zone after the 1967 war with a means to earn their living and help their families. Later knitting machines were purchased to increase production.

Another, larger project, was the Om-Kolthoum House. The project, in Cairo, was to assist families of those killed in combat. Besides workshops, there was a music hall and a music library. Unfortunately Om-Kolthoum did not live to see them completed.

Om-Kolthoum also established and financed a musicians' organization. It was registered in 1942, and in recognition of her efforts, she was elected its head.

Awards and accolades

No other Arab woman artist has earned the awards, decorations and other accolades that Om-Kolthoum has, both nationally and internationally. At home she was one of three eminent artists to win the title "People's Artist," the other two being men. She was also decorated by the governments of Pakistan, Iraq, Lebanon, Jordan, Syria, and Morocco.

She never retired but continued singing until two years before her death in February 1975.

Her funeral was a national event. The huge mourning crowds carried her coffin through some of the main streets of Cairo.

Om-Kolthoum will be remembered as a great woman who brought joy to many hearts and served society in many ways.

Helana Sidaros

Helana Sidaros is a gynecologist and obstetrician who has dedicated her life to medicine and voluntary social work. She belongs to the generation of pioneers, those young women who were educated and went on to work in the first third of the 20th century, when this was an achievement in Egypt.

Family background and early education

Helana was born in 1904 in Tanta, a provincial town, the second child in a family of six. She belonged to a middle-class family, an extended family that lived in a large house. She was a weak child and was not sent to school until she was eight years old. She went to the Coptic Girls' School, one of the earliest schools for girls in the country. This school taught girls until the third grade only. Girls at that time did not take any public examinations, not even those for the primary school certificate.

Helana was a bright child and her father was determined to give her the best education available. After finishing at the Coptic school, she was sent as a boarder to the Saneya School, another early girls' school.

Helana then joined the Teachers' Training College to train to be a teacher, this being the only career available to women at the time. The course was four years. Students were all boarders and the education was free. The head-

Helana (with spectacles) in the operating theater. She was one of the first women in Egypt to be sent abroad to study by the government.

mistress and the teachers were all English except the Arabic teacher who was a sheikh (an Arab scholar trained in religious studies).

A chance to specialize

At the end of her second year at the college, Helana was chosen to go to England to specialize in mathematics, her favorite subject. "I was delighted," she said, "and the family agreed, and so I went."

She was one of the first women to be sent to study in England, as no higher study was then available at home for women. In England she loved the teachers and managed to have a fairly easy life.

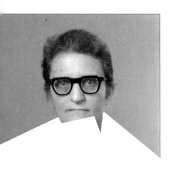

Helana Sidaros was one of the first few women in Egypt to qualify as a doctor.

Helana rebels Helana heard after a while that the training would be limited to attending high school, which was equivalent to the Egyptian secondary school. She would be given a letter at the end of the course to specify her speciality. She found this degrading. So she immediately wrote to the education attaché asking to return home and complete her studies there.

"Within a week," she recalls, "the attaché came to the school and demanded to see me. I thought that I had been granted my request and that I would be sent home....This was not to be. The attaché came to tell me of a new plan and to find out if I approved." The new plan, it turned out, was for her to do medical studies.

In Egypt a new society, the Kitchener Memorial Society, had been formed. One of its plans was to establish a women's hospital for women patients only and run by women doctors. It was decided to start training a team of women doctors in England until doctors could be trained in Egypt.

Helana was told that she was one of the chosen team if she agreed. With her family's consent, Helana accepted the offer. After passing the London matriculation examinations, she was admitted to the London School of Medicine for Women, together with five other Egyptians.

Medical studentship Life as a medical student was enjoyable for Helana. She enjoyed all her subjects except anatomy. Like many male and female students, she found the first weeks of anatomy rather harrowing.

She failed in surgery the first time because of her hazy knowledge of anatomy. However, she took the examination again after six months and passed. Helana qualified as a doctor in 1930, after nine long and hard years, "But it was worth it."

First Egyptian senior resident Dr. Helana Sidaros returned to Egypt to work at the Kitchener Memorial Hospital. There was an English resident doctor who was female and an Egyptian medical staff, all male doctors. When the English resident doctor left, Helana, who had been gaining experience, was thought capable of taking her place as a senior resident.

After four years at the Kitchener Hospital, Helana went on to work at the Welfare Center for the Care of Children. Soon she started a private practice.

She performed operations and deliveries at the Coptic Hospital. "There I grew and worked till I became too old and thought it unfair to my patients to work any more, and so retired," says this dedicated and distinguished medical pioneer.

Amina al-Said

Amina al-Said ("ahl-sa-EED"), the first true Egyptian woman journalist, was born in 1914 and was brought up in Asyut, an Upper Egypt province. Her father was a doctor. Owing to his political involvement in the 1919 Revolution, he was imprisoned. His wife, no less patriotic, used to aid the rebels and give them shelter in the basement of the house.

Amina had one brother and several sisters. They all grew up in the nationalistic atmosphere of the Revolution and amid the call for independence and social reform.

Education Amina's father was proud of his daughters and was determined to give them the best possible education. He wanted them to be "men in dresses," Amina said at one time. He sent Karima, her elder sister, to study in England.

Amina al-Said, journalist, novelist, feminist activist.

Amina was a brave and independent young woman. Against tradition, she went to play tennis in the university stadium. This aroused strong opposition among the male students and faculty. However, as she was determined to play, and it was found that she wore a long-sleeved tennis outfit of reasonable length, she was allowed to do so by the dean.

Then he took the rest of the family to Cairo, where the best opportunities for education were available.

Amina went to one of the best state secondary schools for girls and the first school to offer a course leading to the secondary school certificate. She was one of the third group of young women to go to college and the first to join the Department of English Language and Literature, Cairo University, Fouad I University at the time.

Amina and the Hawa

The *Hawa* appeared in 1954, after two years of preparation. It was an immediate success. The first issue sold 17,000 copies. Sales figures continued to rocket, soon reaching 100,000 copies, an enormous figure for those days.

Amina held her position as editor until 1981. Through this period *Hawa* was a platform for defending women's rights and supporting women in trouble. It reached a broad readership of both men and women. Amina was successful in attracting men to read *Hawa*.

The brave and outspoken editor not only defended women's rights, but also called for radical social reform and wrote political articles. She was criticized and at times fierce attacks were launched against her, but she stood firm. Said Mustafa Amin, her one-time mentor: "She gets out of one crisis to be involved in another. No sooner does a storm subside than another begins. She receives readers' abuse with the same happiness that she receives letters of admiration. She puts up with preachers' curses and revels in attacks and threats, regarding them as flower bouquets."

Press career Amina started her press career in 1932 before she graduated from college. She worked at the *Akher Saa* (*Latest News*). In 1952 she was picked by Emile Zaidan, co-owner of al-Hilal publishing house, to be editor of a new monthly woman's magazine *Hawa* (*Eve*).

In 1956 she became a member of the Press Syndicate Board and in 1959 its chairperson. She was the first woman to become a member of the executive board of al-Hilal, the publisher of *Hawa*. In 1975 she was appointed head of the executive board, a position she retained until she retired in 1981. Since then she has been acting as consultant to al-Hilal.

Committed creative writer Amina al-Said was no less socially and nationally committed as a creative writer than as a journalist. She wrote two novels, *Al-Gamiha* (*The Shrew*) and *Akhir al-Tariq* (*End of the Road*), a collection of short stories, and *Wujouh fi al-Zalam* (*Faces in the Dark*), a collection of articles originally published in her women's page in the *Hawa*. She also wrote a book on Byron, the English romantic poet who fought for the freedom of Greece. She translated Rudyard Kipling's *Jungle Book*, and Louisa May Alcott's *Little Women*, an early sign of her feminist interests. Her only travel book is *Moshahadat fi al-Hind* (*Scenes from India*).

Unlike some people who study foreign languages and literature, she did not neglect her Arabic. She writes beautiful Arabic, simple, vivid and stimulating. Her style is a tool for argument, defensive or aggressive, but always witty and effective. She is also an eloquent and persuasive speaker. Her talent for the language was discovered quite early by a senior inspector who visited her school. So impressed was she with the young girl's Arabic that she provided a teacher of the language to coach her at home.

The Shrew Amina's first novel, *The Shrew*, bears the seeds of her outlook toward life and society. Though it is partly autobiographical, it is strongly marked by the author's detachment.

It presents a panorama of the life of a young Egyptian woman in the '30s and '40s. It is a brilliant rendering of a woman's inner life, her rebelliousness and her final alienation. This novel is widely regarded as a landmark in Egyptian women's writing.

Activist feminist Inspired by the courage of the pioneer feminists, Amina wrote a letter to Hoda Shaarawi in 1932 proposing the establishment of a feminist group for younger women as part of the Egyptian Feminist Union to assist older feminists in their work. Pleased with the idea, Hoda Shaarawi readily agreed to the formation of Shaqiqat (Sisters). Amina became the secretary of the new group.

Struggle with reactionaries Amina is particularly outspoken about the misunderstanding of religion. She is very critical of the regression of the last two decades and the increasing numbers of women who have resumed wearing the veil. She blames women for yielding to reactionary calls.

As member of the Consultative Assembly (1980–1986), she bravely demanded the reform of family laws. At a January 1992 gathering, held in her honor by the Women Writers' Association, of which she is a chairperson, she said she was still willing to lead a demonstration in support of women's demands for the reform of these laws. She is still as staunch a fighter as ever.

Hoda Shaarawi (foreground) with Amina to her left. In 1944 Amina accompanied Hoda Shaarawi on a trip through the Arab countries to call for the establishment of the Arab Feminist Union. Their trip was a success and the Arab Feminist Union was formed in the same year.

Dr. Aisha Rateb chairing a meeting as Minister of Social Affairs and Insurance. As minister, she pushed for changes in the law to provide legal protection for women, as well as equality.

Aisha Rateb

Dr. Aisha Rateb was brought up in a well-to-do family. Her father had his own pharmacy and the family lived in one of the old districts of Cairo. She had a happy childhood. Quite early in her life she said she wanted to be educated and achieve self-fulfillment. Both parents supported her work and her dreams.

Education At school Aisha loved mathematics and languages. After finishing primary school, she went to one of the best girls' secondary schools.

In 1945 she went to Cairo University where she studied law. Four years later, at the age of 21, she graduated among the top six in her class.

Seeking employment Aisha qualified for a junior post at the High Administrative Court, but was denied appointment, on the basis that she was a woman. This was regarded as discrimination against women, and the Egyptian Feminist Union took the case to court. However, it did not go very far.

Aisha then concentrated on pursuing a higher diploma course in law. When a number of law instructors' posts were advertised, she applied. Her application was met with fierce opposition by faculty officials at first. After much deliberation, however, a committee was formed to interview this female candidate. She was found suitable for the post and was appointed in 1950. This was both a personal achievement and a step forward for Egyptian women. Another male preserve was conquered by this determined young woman.

First woman law professor In 1955 Aisha was awarded the Ph.D. degree, a prerequisite for a university lectureship. This was soon followed by her appointment to a lectureship at the Sudan Branch of Cairo University, which was being established at the time.

In 1971 she was made professor, and soon after, the chairman of the Department of International Law, also in Cairo University. She was the first Egyptian woman to occupy these positions.

In politics In 1971 Aisha ran for the elections of the central committee of the Arab Socialist Union Party, the only party at the time. She won the second largest number of votes. She was also a member of the New Constitution Committee (the committee responsible for drawing up the 1971 constitution which provided for a multi-party system of government).

Cabinet minister Aisha was appointed Minister of Social Affairs in 1971, the second Egyptian woman to be appointed to this post. In 1975 she was given the Insurance portfolio in addition to that of Social Affairs.

As a senior cabinet minister, Aisha chaired several important cabinet committees, such as the legislative committee, the supplies committee and the development committee. She was also a member of the Family Planning Higher Council.

As Minister of Insurance, Aisha was responsible for many important changes in the social insurance laws. She established the Insurance Organization to implement social insurance for non-governmental workers.

New insurance policy

Fully aware of the importance of legal protection and equality for women and eager to assist them to positively contribute to society, Aisha undertook several changes in laws regarding working women and women in general. New advantages to women were legalized. Some of them are listed below:

- The right of the wife to her dead husband's pension even if he was 60 and she 40 or over at the time of their marriage. This was an amendment to an earlier law that deprived a woman 40 years and over who married a man over 60 of the right to his pension.
- The right of a divorcee to a pension from her ex-husband in case of being divorced against her will and in case the marriage lasted 20 years, provided she did not remarry and had no income of her own.
- The right of a widow to her husband's pension and her own.
- The right of a mother to her children's share of their father's pension after they marry.
- The right of a daughter or sister to a man's pension as long as she was not married or did not work.
- The right of a daughter or sister to claim the pension of the father or brother after his death, without prejudice to the rights of others entitled to it, if she was divorced or widowed.
  So popular was this new insurance policy to a large sector of society that Dr. Aisha Rateb was said to have "brought a smile to every home in Egypt."

Aisha Rateb just before presenting her credentials as ambassador to Denmark. She was Egypt's first woman ambassador.

Decade Conference in 1980. She provided great support to the Egyptian delegation.

In 1981 she was appointed ambassador to West Germany and retained the post until 1984. She then returned to Cairo University as Professor Emeritus.

As ambassador she was a credit to her country. In Copenhagen, she recalled, when she first presented her credentials, "everyone came to see the woman ambassador from Africa." After taking up office in West Germany, where there were no women ambassadors, she made such a good impression that one diplomat said, "It is time we had a lady ambassador."

Aisha undertook her diplomatic responsibilities with remarkable competence. She said she often had to work from seven o'clock in the morning until after midnight. She was keen on presenting a true image of Egypt. She visited universities, received Danish and German students at her residence, held receptions and organized exhibitions of ancient Egyptian monuments and modern art. She was active in bringing members of various diplomatic missions together. Her knowledge of foreign languages and international law was a great asset.

Apart from her political and diplomatic career, she has contributed to voluntary welfare work and is a

First Egyptian woman ambassador In 1977 Aisha left the ministry and resumed her position as professor of law at Cairo University. In 1979 she was appointed first Egyptian woman ambassador, a historic achievement for Egyptian women. She took office in Denmark and was in Copenhagen during the International Women's

member of various law associations. Some time during her career she married, and she has two grown-up sons. She says she had no difficulty managing her double roles.

Aida Gindy

Aida Gindy is a remarkable woman who dedicated her entire life to social work both nationally and internationally. Her childhood experience shaped her life and outlook. Her mother was a woman who served the community, particularly in the church, and supported specific causes such as the rights of women in the social and political spheres. Aida grew up in this kind of background.

First welfare program Her interest in social welfare developed while she was still in secondary school. She and a group of students got together to promote summer school for children from poorer districts of Cairo. The first school was held in the garden of her grandfather's house. The students devoted their whole vacation to organizing literacy classes, craft making and setting up a small-scale cooperative stall where children could sell their products in the neighborhood. The program included educational visits to museums and other places of historical interest as well as to villages on the outskirts of the city.

The idea was taken up by Aida's junior college, which opened its doors during the summer vacations. "This," she recalled, "helped many students of the college to develop a genuine concern for community action."

Aida Gindy, a remarkable woman who has dedicated her life to social work.

Interest in rural life During the war, Aida went to the home of social worker Aziza Hussain, in the village. "At that time, I got to say this is what I am going to do, human interest, human development," she said in an interview. Aida Gindy and her fellow university students became exposed to the problems of rural women and children. Interest in social service started in earnest at that time. "Upbringing and schooling encouraged this kind of work, together with the enthusiasm of youth. One is encouraged and inspired," she says.

Studying sociology Aida studied sociology at the American University in Cairo and obtained her B.A. degree in 1945. At the end of 1946 she applied for a scholarship and was granted one to study social economics and social work in the United States at Bryn Mawr College in Pennsylvania. She was the first Egyptian woman with a degree in social work to go to the United States.

Aida and the United Nations The United Nations was born in 1946, and while in the United States, Aida studied its charter. She also read the debates. "I wanted to know what the UN was all about."

Through her professor, who was an advisor to the UN and was impressed by Aida's work, she became an intern at the world body during the summer months. Meanwhile, she had obtained her M.A. degree and done the credits for a Ph.D. She would have easily fulfilled the remaining requirements. But there were priorities to consider and the UN came first. She became a trainee at the UN from 1948 to 1949. This was to be the beginning of a long and valued career with the UN. "This was the beginning of my interest globally. The ideals of the UN became an obsession with me," she says.

Aida Gindy was offered a job in the UN Social Development Unit. Though she enjoyed her work at the UN, she never forgot Egypt. It was at this point that she said she wanted to go back home and "put my head at the reality of things."

In 1950 she returned to Egypt where she worked with the Ministry of Social Affairs for two years. But in 1952, she was offered another post at the UN. Although her work was valued at home, she was advised to accept the post. Not only was it good to have an Egyptian woman at the UN, but more importantly, she would be helping other countries as well. So, late that year, she joined the Social Welfare Section at UN headquarters in New York. "[The] United Nations at the time was a great

Unit chief of social welfare for Africa

With the establishment of the Economic Commission for Africa in Addis Ababa, Ethiopia, in 1958, Aida had an opportunity to go to Africa, when its nations were beginning to gain independence. Aida, as unit chief, was in charge of 10 African countries.

She was reappointed to the Commission for two years, but she stayed for three. She was the only woman seconded from headquarters. Between 1959 and 1963, she helped to establish the Social Development Division.

Of her experience with the Commission, she says, "This marked the high point of my professional work with the UN. It was clear to me from the beginning of my experience in the region that the program of the Commission had to focus attention on women in Africa."

She traveled all over Africa to assist the newly independent states in social development.

Aida returned to UN headquarters after the three years in Ethiopia. From 1966 to 1975 she was in charge of the Social Welfare Service Section for Africa.

inspiration. I was trained by people committed to human equality, human rights, international exchange of services, family and child welfare, social security, better housing, health education and rural development," she says.

UNICEF In 1975 UNICEF discovered that they had no senior woman in the program for East Africa. They asked that Aida be appointed regional director in Africa. She was stationed in Nairobi, Kenya, and was in charge of 20 countries. It was a big responsibility.

In 1980 UNICEF headquarters appointed Aida the regional director of all Europe. For a woman from the Third World, this was a great achievement. Aida had proved her competence and dedication to human development during her sojourn in Africa.

As UNICEF director, Aida was involved in community participation, fund raising, program planning and policy making among other things.

Active in Egypt In 1984, after an active involvement in global work, Aida returned to Egypt to devote more of her time to national social work. "After 32 years of international work, I am very happy to be involved nationally and to serve my country," she says. However, she remains consultant to UNICEF.

In Egypt Aida is active in both official

and voluntary capacities. She was the Egyptian government delegate to the Women's Decade Conference in Nairobi in 1985. She later became a member of the advisory board of the National Council for Childhood and Motherhood. She is involved with the Integrated Care Society, which undertakes voluntary work for improving school life for Egyptian children. Aida is also a member of the Egyptian Association of Friends of Children's Libraries, which promotes the establishment of children's libraries both in rural and urban areas.

A poor part of Cairo. It is for the social development of the people in her country and of Africa that Aida Gindy worked during the years as UN unit chief of social welfare for Africa.

chapter six

A Lifetime

A fter looking at women's participation in society in general, it is time to examine more closely the successive stages of a woman's life. In this chapter we will look at the different stages of a woman's lifetime, from childhood to old age, highlighting moments of particular significance. Like those of women elsewhere, the roles of women in Egypt are changing with the passage of time.

Birth and the girl child

"Congratulations! It's a lovely girl." The father rushes in to see his wife and the baby girl. The mother anxiously asks if he is disappointed that it is not a boy and he reassures her, adding that the next time it will probably be a boy. All the family—grandparents, uncles, aunts, cousins—crowd around to see the baby and to discuss whether she resembles her mother or father.

Parents like to have both a son and a daughter. If they have two daughters in a row, they hope the next baby, if they decide to have another, will be a boy. If they already have a son, they hope to have a daughter. At one point, and in some rural areas still, parents would continue trying to have a son even after six or seven girls. With family planning fast becoming the norm among educated families, two or three children, whether boys or girls, is the general pattern.

A Nubian villager with her grandchild (*opposite*) and two young sisters (*right*). In a lifetime, from childhood to old age, the woman takes on many different roles in society.

A LIFETIME 99

seeds, nuts and sweets are symbols of fertility, wisdom, and a happy life. Then the children, followed by the adults, are given a lit candle each. They follow the mother around the house, singing a song particular to this occasion. The song wishes the baby to grow up to be like those who are carrying the candles and singing.

Childhood

First birthday This is quite an event. Not only children but close relatives and friends are invited to the celebration of a child's first birthday. If by good fortune the child can walk by then, a bicycle is a welcome present. The house is decorated with balloons and the one-year-old is given lots of presents. Photographs are taken, and with sweets, cookies and candies, the children have the time of their life. Blowing out the one candle on the birthday cake marks the height of the excitement. By then the little girl is exhausted and ready for bed.

Nursery school When the girl is one or two years old, the mother may decide to go back to work. The girl may be left each morning with one of her grand-mothers or at a day care center until the parents feel it is time for her to go to a nursery school. Children go to a nursery school from the age of two until they are ready to join a preschool class at the age of four or five. Nursery school hours

Fridays are when children get to spend the day with their parents, who may take them to an amusement park.

First few days of life In the first few days of a baby's life, she is visited by family members and friends of the family. Each bears a gift: a gold talisman, clothes, toys or money. The immediate family helps out by bringing food. The little girl is picked up, kissed and joggled by every visitor. Her mother breast-feeds her and plans for the traditional party given for the baby one week after her birth for kin and friends.

The seventh-day party On the day of the party the house is packed with friends and relatives. The traditional rites take place. The baby is placed in a grain sifter on top of a layer of seeds, nuts and sweets. She is gently shaken by the grandmother or an elderly friend, while someone bangs on a brass pot to give the little girl a brave heart. The

are generally from 7 a.m. to 4 p.m., but children do not always stay the whole time; how long they stay depends on their mothers' working hours.

At school the girl enjoys the companionship of boys and girls of her age. She learns to draw, sing and play games with other children.

Fridays are special. Both parents have the day off and they spend the day together, sometimes having lunch with the rest of the family (grandparents, uncles, aunts and cousins). Occasionally they go out for the day.

Children's entertainment Egyptian radio and television broadcast various programs for children. For preschool children they include cartoons and musicals.

For older children, programs are more varied, aiming at both amusement and education. Girls and boys often take part in staging a short play or presenting a dance on these programs. School children are encouraged to participate in such programs.

Some cinemas hold special morning shows for children on vacation.

Children's decade

Concern for children, especially of the less privileged sectors of the society, has recently led to a number of measures. The years 1988 to 1997 have been declared a children's decade by President Hosni Mubarak. Largely through the efforts of Mrs. Suzan Mubarak, wife of the President, 1990 saw the implementation of an illiteracy eradication project in five villages.

In 1991 a number of centers for handicapped children were set up. At these centers medical, social and educational facilities are provided. In 1992 the attention was turned to rural children: more libraries for children were founded in various parts of the country, and youth centers and rural clubs were set up.

School outing. Boys and girls may go to the same school at primary level, but at the preparatory and secondary levels, they usually go to single-sex schools.

Schooling and discipline

Children, both boys and girls, usually spend two years in kindergarten, from about four to six years of age. Some children have already been to nursery school and are accustomed to school life.

At the age of six, there is another important event for the child: starting primary school. This is when school-work begins in earnest. Classes are crowded, play and activity time are limited. Homework becomes routine and parents give a hand in the process of learning.

Some primary schools are mixed, others are not. On the whole, there is no segregation of boys and girls at this stage in terms of curriculum. Boys and girls receive the same attention and follow the same courses. School discipline does not reflect any sexual stereotyping of roles. Mixed schools are more common at the primary level than at the preparatory level and rare at the secondary level.

To have a hobby, the girl may take lessons outside of school: dancing, music, drawing or sports. Some girls may be allowed to choose and to participate, but this is not the case for all girls. They are not always given the chance to have such interests.

Little girls are encouraged to help their mothers with easy household chores and they often like being useful. Elder sisters like to play mother to younger brothers and sisters.

Boys are to some extent being encouraged to help around in the house, mainly in urban areas.

Adolescence

Adolescence coincides partly with preparatory, partly with secondary school. Going through a difficult phase of life adjusting to changes as she grows from childhood into adulthood, a teenage girl may be restless and sensitive and sometimes touchy.

At school some girls may have a crush on one of the teachers, male or female. The girl confides her secrets to a best friend rather than to her mother. At home she keeps mostly to herself.

Teenagers are active, playing sports, participating in activity clubs at school or college such as music, drama or crafts clubs. Some teenagers involve themselves in voluntary welfare work.

Like teenagers elsewhere, the Egyptian teenage girl goes through a difficult phase of adjusting to the changes in her life as she grows from childhood into adulthood.

Piano for girls

At one time, playing the piano was a skill that every girl who could afford it had to acquire. It was widely regarded as an asset in marriage in the middle and upper classes. Parents would boast of their daughter's exquisite piano playing.

With girls going to school and college, then working, they no longer have the time to spend on such things, unless they make time for it. Nowadays a girl learns to play the piano only when she really wants to do so. She plays as a child, perhaps. But by the time she reaches the last year of secondary school or goes to college, she has little time for it.

Science or arts?

After the first year of secondary school, a girl's future becomes a topic of discussion for the family. Everyone voices his or her view, even though each claims to be open-minded enough to let the girl make her own decision. The debate is essentially whether she should choose to follow a science or arts course. A science course will eventually lead to a career in medicine, engineering or pure science, while an arts course will probably lead to a career as a teacher, lawyer, accountant or secretary.

The general view is that a career in the sciences is more demanding. Due consideration must also be given to the fact that the girl will eventually get married and have children and must be free to give priority to her family, as good child care centers for the very young are scarce.

In 1991, out of a total of 86,658 students taking science courses in secondary schools, 30,900 or 35.6% were girls.

Secondary school experience

After five years of primary school, 12-year-olds go through three years of preparatory school, after which they go through another three years of secondary school before they choose whether or not to go to college.

Ambitious students take the three years of secondary school seriously, particularly the final year—students are given places in different departments at different universities according to their examination results. Those who want to be doctors and engineers must study very hard as the departments of medicine and engineering only accept students with top marks.

Girls who do not go on to college go to technical training institutes to train for a vocation. Some girls take short courses in typing, shorthand or computer as a quick way of finding a job.

About one-third of all college students are female.

In the rural areas quite a few girls drop out of school after the preparatory stage. They stay at home and are prepared for marriage and raising a family. Some go to work. However, girls in the rural areas are increasingly continuing their education and going to college, then working.

College years

For most girls, college will be their first experience with coeducation. This is also true of most male students. The first weeks of the first term will, therefore, be a period of adaption to the new life. Tentative steps are taken on both sides to approach each other. Some students, whether male or female, are rather timid, and they will keep mostly to their own friends, at first. But groups soon form and an atmosphere of comradeship is created. For students studies soon take up most of their time and energy. Everyone enjoys the sense of freedom marking college life, but this does not diminish their eagerness for absorbing new knowledge and meeting the challenge of college studies.

It is mostly the good students who participate in social, cultural and sporting activities. They seem to possess the energy for both academic work and enjoying themselves. Such activities bring students together, perhaps more than the lectures, the research work or the practical classes, where a spirit of competition exists between the boys and girls. As time passes, however, friendships grow among them. For some, friendships turn into more intimate relationships. Some marriages eventually result from these relationships.

Student matches Marriage is often in the cards for a young college woman.

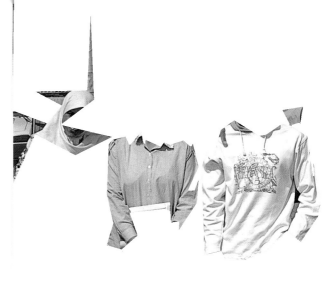

Quite a few girls get engaged halfway through their degree program. Some get engaged to their fellow students. Some even get married and have their first baby while still at college. It is interesting to note how anxious such young women are to continue with their studies even after marriage and having to take care of the household. More often, however, having a baby is postponed until after graduation.

Most parents insist that their daughters graduate first before marriage. As a rule, young women themselves prefer to wait, to have time to think what they want to do with their lives before becoming wives and mothers and taking on more responsibilities.

Students at Cairo University. For many students college is their first experience with coeducation.

Assistant front desk manager of a hotel. For young Egyptian women, work and economic independence are becoming more important.

More often, at the beginning of her working career at least, she continues to be the recipient of spending money, plus money for clothes and extras. This, of course, depends on the economic level of the family.

Making job choices Despite the recent call for women to stay at home, and a degree of reluctance of some businesses to employ women, many jobs are open to them.

Ambitious and achievement-oriented women select the more demanding jobs. This means meeting challenges of creative, hard work and male competition and, sometimes, prejudice too. However, with initiative and a readiness to learn and adapt, some manage to reach the top rungs of management. Women in managerial positions and on executive boards of large businesses or government departments are no longer novelties.

Those who plan to get married immediately after graduation are often satisfied with temporary or less demanding jobs. They want the best of both worlds: married life and a comfortable job.

Special classes A girl often finds it useful to attend classes in typing, shorthand or computer skills, which may prove useful when applying for a job or for advancement in her career. Dress-

Working girl

Going to work is the stage in the life of an Egyptian girl which marks her entry into the world. Having a job automatically means economic independence. A working girl generally keeps her salary, unless the family needs a helping hand. Sometimes a young working girl becomes the breadwinner for the family, undertaking this responsibility until she marries, or until a younger member of the family is able to do so.

making or home economics are only taken up if a young woman has more spare time, or if she is thinking of settling down as a housewife.

Art and craft classes are becoming popular with a small minority of young women with artistic inclinations and sufficient spare time. Besides enjoying their hobby, they can sell their products if they are good.

Freedom versus social tradition

Despite the increasingly greater freedom acquired by women, a working girl mostly abides by common tradition. Unmarried working girls continue to live with their families unless they work in a different part of the country. If they do, they keep close contacts with their families and spend weekends and/or holidays with them. Otherwise they enjoy a greater degree of freedom and independence than those who live at home.

Dating is not very common among Egyptian girls. Young men and women go out in groups, or they meet at college, clubs and at work. Otherwise, unless there is some kind of commitment to an engagement leading to marriage, it is rather unacceptable for a girl to go out frequently with a young man.

Sports Today more girls engage in sports in their spare time. With the falling of barriers between the woman and the outside world, she can choose the sport she likes, such as swimming, basketball or tennis. Girls play sports in sports clubs, college stadiums or state youth centers.

Welfare work For a socially-motivated young woman, the time after graduation and before marriage may be the best time to take an interest in voluntary work. She becomes a member of one of the various women's associations involved in community service, social, cultural or religious. She either takes after her mother, aunt or grandmother who participated in voluntary work, or is motivated by a personal urge. She devotes much of her time to such projects as organizing camps for deprived women or children, caring for elderly people, promoting family planning in rural areas, or combating pollution in the cities.

A young woman continues welfare work until she marries and starts a family of her own. Owing to the lack of time, she gradually withdraws from such associations, suspending her membership until the children are older and need less attention.

Pursuing further studies An ambitious young woman may not be satisfied with a college degree and a job. She may decide to pursue further studies in her field of specialization.

Motives vary from one individual to another. She may wish to fill in the time before marriage, to improve her professional status, or simply satisfy her love of knowledge.

Organizing camps for deprived girls

A popular kind of activity with the Young Women's Christian Association, whose membership includes both Moslem and Christian women, is organizing summer camps for girls from orphanages or girls' homes. They take them to the seaside to give them a holiday as well as to teach them a few simple crafts to generate income, such as basket-making and knitting.

These programs offer an opportunity for consciousness-raising as well as initiation in some practical and useful interests. The benefit these girls gain from the company of educated young women is considerable.

For the volunteers themselves, the project is no less satisfying in terms of a sense of achievement and self-fulfillment.

Being single

Most Egyptian women marry. Single women seem to be more common among educated women, either because they have higher standards or they find their studies or careers so rewarding that they pass up the opportunity to marry. As young women, they mostly live with their families. Later on in life, with the death of their parents, they often live with unmarried brothers. If there are no unmarried brothers, they either live with a married brother or sister or on their own.

In the old days, when far fewer women were educated and employed, and consequently less self-reliant, a brother would often remain unmarried and devote his life to looking after his unmarried sister or sisters.

With increasing education and employment opportunities, women are becoming more independent and can be trusted to look after themselves. Being a single woman is no longer a deterrent to a full life. The word "spinster" has completely lost its unpleasant innuendoes.

As for socializing with men and women of their own age, a single woman enjoys the same opportunities as a married woman.

While most Egyptian women marry, being single is no longer viewed as an undesirable state, and many single women lead full lives.

Marriages among relatives

Marriages among relatives are still common in rural areas and among less-educated sectors of society. The matchmaking is often undertaken by parents or relatives. The dominant pattern is marriages between cousins: between a woman and her father's brother's son or, less frequently, mother's sister's son.

Often, especially in extended families, the children grow up together, and the parents feel reassured about their daughters when they marry blood relatives. The family tie is regarded as a kind of safeguard against the possible problems of married life.

Among some well-to-do families, it is a means of keeping property in the family. However, such marriages are increasingly disappearing.

Courtship and engagement

When two young people get to know each other and decide to marry, the young man approaches the girl's father. To pave the way, the young woman usually tells her mother, who in her turn tells the father. The father agrees to meet the young man, and if he likes him, he approves of the match. Then both the young man and his family visit the girl's family and make a formal marriage proposal.

This is generally followed by a period of courtship preceding the formal engagement celebration. The two young people meet either at home in the company of the family, or go out together, depending on the family traditions.

Engagement celebration When both the young people and the families feel that things are going well, they set a date for the engagement to be formally announced. This is a religious ceremony, usually followed by a reception for family and close friends. For a Moslem

Matchmaking

The traditional matchmaker is becoming rare. She is called upon only when some more conventional families find difficulty in marrying off their children. This is particularly true where a certain degree of sex segregation still exists.

Some kinds of matchmaking have not completely disappeared, however. Friends, relatives, colleagues and even bosses often play the role of matchmaker. When they think that two young people will make a nice couple, either because they share the same interests or because they share the same background, they set out to bring them together. They drop a hint here and another there, praising the young woman to the young man or the other way around. Sometimes they arrange a meeting, which is made to appear unplanned. If that is well taken by the parties concerned, the friends make no secret of their matchmaking intentions, and discreetly withdraw, leaving the young people to carry on as they will.

An engaged couple. Young people in Egypt generally do not go out on single dates until the man has made a marriage proposal and the girl's parents have approved the match.

girl, the reading of al-Fatiha (the first text of the Koran) takes place in the young woman's home. For a Christian, the ceremony is performed in church or at home.

Engagement gifts The young man gives the girl an engagement gift, generally a diamond ring or another piece of jewelry, in addition to the traditional wedding ring. The girl wears the wedding ring on the third finger of her right hand until the wedding, when it is moved to the third finger of the left hand.

At the reception, sherbet is offered to the guests, before tea or a buffet dinner. There is usually music and sometimes a traditional singer and a dancer, or modern dancing.

With greater opportunities for young men and women to be together, love matches are increasingly becoming more common as well as more acceptable in Egyptian society. Young people meet at college and in the workplace, apart from social functions and gatherings. In the university student societies play a significant role in bringing young people together.

Apartment blocks in Cairo. Looking for a place to set up home can be quite a daunting experience for young people in the cities where there is a housing shortage.

Marriage preparations

After the engagement, an agreement regarding the furnishing of the young couple's future home is reached and the date for the wedding is set. According to Moslem traditions, the young man pays a certain amount of money, called *mahr* ("MA-hr," dowry), usually spent on furnishing the new home. As for Christians, an agreement is struck based on mutual understanding and cooperation. In both cases, it is common for the families to assist the young people to start their new life.

The first thing the young couple have to think about and plan for is where to live. Owing to a shortage of housing in the cities and the phenomenal prices of apartments, finding an apartment is no easy matter. If they are lucky they will find an apartment within a few months.

In the cities couples sometimes live with their parents, but most couples prefer to live on their own right from the beginning of their married life. If they do live with their parents at the beginning, whether they live with the woman's or the man's parents depends on which family can accommodate them. Young couples either rent or buy their apartment. At one time more people rented their apartments, but increasingly owning one's home is becoming the norm for those who can afford it.

In the rural areas, young couples more often live with the young man's family. Sometimes an extra room or two are specially built for them. Some couples not only begin married life by living with the man's parents, but continue to do so until the home becomes their own, particularly in the case of eldest sons.

The wedding

The arrangements for the wedding are made by the young people and their families. Invitations have to be sent out after the locations for both the wedding ceremony and the reception are confirmed.

For the woman, there is the trousseau to see to, and above all, her wedding gown, as well as dresses for the maids of honor.

Moslem ceremony The Moslem wedding ceremony, Katb al-Kitab, or the signing of the contract, is performed between the father of the bride, or someone representing him, and the groom, in the presence of the Mazoun ("MAHzon," an official authorized to perform marriages) and two witnesses. It takes place either at the mosque or in the family home of the bride. This is followed by a wedding reception for friends and relatives to announce the marriage to them. Receptions can be elaborate or simple affairs, either held in the man's family home or at a hotel or club.

In the countryside all the people in the village are invited to a big feast at the groom's parents' home following the ceremony. Even the poorest family will try to put on a show, sometimes going into debt to pay for it.

Christian ceremony Christian weddings are held in church. The church is specially decorated with flowers for the occasion. As the guests enter the church, each is given a small bonbonière containing a chocolate and some sugar-coated almonds. It is tied up with a colored ribbon holding a small card which has on it the names of the bride and the groom and the wedding date.

The bridal procession moves to the altar accompanied by music and women's *zaghrouda* (trilling sounds). After the couple have exchanged vows and signed the marriage register, and after a number of prayers and hymns, the procession moves to the church door, again accompanied by music and *zaghrouda*. At the door the newlyweds and their parents receive congratulations and good wishes from relatives and friends.

The wedding reception is held on the same day either at the groom's home or at a hotel or club. It is much the same as that of a Moslem wedding. Sometimes the reception is held at the time of the engagement and not after the wedding ceremony.

A Moslem wedding couple arriving at their reception in a hotel. Receptions can be simple or elaborate affairs depending on what the couple can afford.

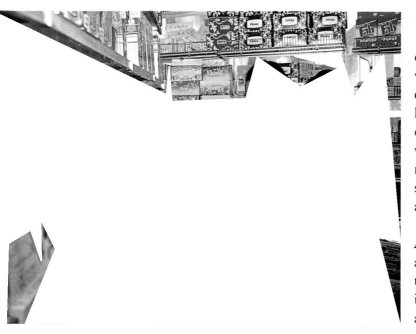

especially with young men married to working women, there are signs of a changed attitude. Men are willing to help if they can, for example, they will do the shopping or look after the baby while the mother is busy. If they are really ultra-modern, they may fix a simple meal or at least do the dishes after a meal.

Absentee husbands In Egypt many male agricultural workers have had to leave their farms to seek work in the cities or in nearby oil countries. When the men are away on a long-term basis, the women have additional duties. The wife has to cope on her own with looking after the children and often seeing to the farm as well.

The absentee husbands generally work hard and send money and presents home. They often return home to see the family during holidays. Only rarely do they fail to send money home or to return home at all. Sometimes when the man comes home with a lot of money he may be tempted to take another wife. More often the men build a house for their family or start a business to improve the standard of living for wife and children.

Rural women who are married to agricultural workers are generally more affected by the migrant worker pattern than urban wives who often accompany their husbands going to work abroad.

Above: Shopping for groceries. Marriage marks the beginning of a new life for a woman as she sets up her own home with her husband. She finds herself doing things she has hardly done before, especially if she has lived at home before now—like cooking or shopping for groceries.

Opposite: Young mothers today face the dilemma of whether to give up their jobs to take care of the children or to continue to work.

Wife, working woman

Marriage marks the beginning of a new life for the young bride. It means a new role and status. There will be responsibilities and obligations toward her husband, the household and in-laws. Adapting to her new lifestyle is both exciting and demanding.

Naturally her husband and home come first, but as a working woman, she has to face her dual roles of wife and working woman. If she is lucky, she might have some household help in the first few months of her married life, until she is fully adapted to her dual roles. Household help is common, but it is becoming more expensive.

In Egypt it is not often that men help out with housework. Most men think it is unmanly to do so, but recently,

Being mother

With the prospective additional role of mother, things can become rather hectic for a young working wife. It is time to consider options. Should she give up her job and devote herself entirely to her husband and children? Giving up her job will not only have an impact on the family income at a time when expenses are expected to go up, but it will deprive her of a source of enrichment for her life. It is particularly at this crossroads in her life that the division of labor in the family seems rather unfair, and having to make a choice is really difficult.

In rural areas having a baby and looking after it is regarded as the most natural thing for a wife. In the extended family there are many helping hands to look after the child while the mother does the housework or works on the farm.

In the cities, most children are delivered in maternity hospitals. There are free government hospitals as well as private hospitals. In the rural areas, there are state health units which provide child delivery facilities. At one time midwives delivered babies in most rural areas, and they still do in many villages.

The first baby's arrival marks another new and very significant phase in a woman's life. The joy a newborn baby brings to the whole family, parents and grandparents, is unequalled. Discrimina-

Old Egyptian sayings reflect two attitudes toward girl babies. According to one, this is how a mother feels: "When they said it was a girl, I felt the hut collapse over my head; when they said it was a boy, my back straightened and stiffened." On the other hand, another saying expresses this wisdom: "A daughter is her mother's beloved."

tion between boy and girl at this stage is almost non-existent. Although traditionally families would like a boy, a girl is equally welcome, especially for the first baby.

Planning for a baby

Many young Egyptian wives choose to keep their jobs after the arrival of children.

There are a few options open to a woman who wants to keep her job after childbirth. She can send her baby to a day care center, but day care facilities for young babies are rather rare; most day care centers take children from the age of one or two. Or she can rely on her mother or mother-in-law to look after the baby while she is at work. Finally, she may take advantage of the facilities provided by law for mothers with babies. After the three-month paid maternity leave, she can take unpaid leave to look after the baby for a year and then send the child to a day care center or the grandmother after that.

Mothers breast-feed their children until they are one year old. Some time during the second half of the year, the baby is given some baby food, side by side with breast-feeding. There are very few cases in which a mother cannot breast-feed her baby, but these are the exceptions.

Staying home to look after the baby for whatever length of time depends on the social context and the income of the family. Generally a woman has a rest after delivering a baby. According to an old tradition, the length of this rest is 40 days, but this is no longer always the case.

Women working for the government sometimes take no-pay leave for a year or two to look after their children, if they can afford it. Women working in the private sector generally stay at home only during the period of paid maternity

Egyptian society values the mother's role as the nurturer of future generations. This is reflected in their songs and poems and in the religious celebration of Mother's Day.

leave, which is usually three months. Today some young mothers prefer to stay at home until their children go to a day care center at the age of one or two, then return to work.

Mother's role and society The mother's role is deeply valued by society. One official report contains this pronouncement: "Mother's love nurtures and feeds children. She bears the responsibility of raising them and plays a vital role in shaping their personality. She plants in them the right values and principles and trains them to be good human beings and useful members of society."

Many Egyptian songs express the reciprocal feelings of children for their mothers. Mother's Day on March 21 is religiously celebrated in Egypt.

The public view of the mother, repeatedly voiced at such celebrations, is that the future of society lies in the hands of the mother, since she bears the greatest responsibility in raising its children. According to a wise man, the rearing of a child should start 20 years before its birth, by educating the mother, since she is the first mentor; in fact she is the great school which shapes a strong and sound nature. The great Egyptian poet Ahmad Shawqi has written a memorable line of poetry to this effect: "The mother is a school. If you prepare her well, you will have laid the foundations of a good nation."

A fishing family. Egypt faces an overpopulation problem, particularly in the rural areas, and efforts are made to educate the women on family planning.

Mother's health care Convinced of the need to provide mothers and mothers-to-be with health care, the government is consolidating and developing mother and child care centers. These centers offer services such as health care during pregnancy and care for minor diseases; dental care and treatment for pregnant women and mothers at the dental units of health centers; transfer of serious pregnancy cases and difficult deliveries to hospitals; and sound health care for the mother during pregnancy and after delivery.

Family planning programs Family planning programs are being intensified in an attempt to reduce the problem of overpopulation. Television programs addressing both urban and rural women are made very attractive. The importance of the mother's need of a rest between one pregnancy and another is emphasized, side by side with the baby's need for a longer time in the mother's care. Young wives are shown participating in discussions on the importance of family planning. An attempt is made to involve husbands too.

Divorce

To protect women against divorce, the most disruptive factor of family life, reform of personal status laws has been one of the most important items of feminist demands. Both the wife and children suffer as a result of divorce. Although according to recent studies the rates of divorce in Egypt are decreasing, in most cases it is the man who initiates divorce. In addition, it is easier for a man to divorce his wife than it is for a woman to divorce her husband. A wife has to go to court to get a divorce, and court procedures can take years.

Personal status law reform

The '70s and '80s witnessed significant changes in the area of personal status law. This was the result of the concentrated and continuing canvassing of women's associations and parliamentary women as well as the support of Mrs. Jihan Sadat, wife of the late President Anwar Sadat.

In 1979 personal status laws stipulated the following:

- The right of a woman to a divorce if her husband marries another wife without her consent.
- The wife is to be informed in case of divorce, and is to have custody of the children until boys are 10 and girls 12 years of age.
- The right of the wife to alimony as well as the right to remain in the family home until she remarries or until the period of custody of the children expires.

However, owing to some opposition and controversy over the implementation of these stipulations, particularly regarding the wife's remaining in the family home after the divorce, the legality of the laws was challenged; the laws were first suspended and then declared unconstitutional.

In 1985 new laws were issued stipulating that the wife no longer has the automatic right to divorce if her husband marries again. She can apply for divorce only if she can prove that she suffers from material or moral damage as a result of her husband's having another wife. Moreover, in the case of a second marriage, the husband must provide adequate lodging for the first wife while she has custody of the children.

Growing old

As the years pass the children grow up, and the woman can no longer give them protection or help them make choices. They must proceed on their own. She can only hope that the love and training that she and their father have given them will guide them along the way.

One by one, the children begin to think of marriage and having families of their own. The woman is happy and looks forward to welcoming their spouses and caring for their children. However, her happiness is mixed with anxiety and a bit of sadness at the thought of being separated from them. She can only wish them joy and pray for their happiness. They promise to and do keep in contact, and she is satisfied.

The excitement of having grandchildren

The birth of the first baby of the new generation, the first grandchild, is a very special event. As grandmother, the woman can spoil her first grandchild and those who follow to her heart's content. She will babysit, tell stories and play games with them.

A new life Once the children are grown up and getting on with their lives, the woman has time to renew old interests. She begins to reactivate social, cultural and voluntary activities for which the family and a career had left little time and energy. She resumes membership in women's associations. Greater involvement in welfare work starts to occupy much of her spare time and enhances her sense of participation in the active life of the community.

Her experience and knowledge gained through a full life are valued by younger women. She enjoys the respect of others and more importantly the feeling of being useful. With fewer financial responsibilities, she can afford to travel and tour places she dreamed of seeing but never had the time or the money for with growing family responsibilities.

It is not uncommon for aging parents to live on their own. Except in some rural areas, where the extended family is still the norm, the parents live on their own. If the woman is left alone after the death of her husband, sometimes a grandson moves in to live with her to keep her company and provide a sense of security, besides seeing to her needs. These are the years when she can relax and enjoy the peace and quiet of her own home side by side with the loving attention and care of her children.

In the countryside, old women live in an extended household and share their lives with their children and grandchildren. Life is still busy for the rural grandmother, what with looking after grandchildren and helping with the household chores, but most of her work on the farm and in the house is taken over by daughters-in-law. She is loved and respected and her wisdom is greatly valued by younger members of the household.

Two older women on a shopping trip. Not a few Egyptian women choose to live alone after the death of their husband rather than with married children.

Children in Egypt keep in close contact with their parents even after marriage. If the grandmother is caring for her grandchildren, the little ones will spend the day at her home. However, despite attempts to fill her time, a degree of loneliness is inevitable for the grandmother. Unless she has retained contact with some old friends and colleagues of her own age, life can be lonesome.

Homes for the elderly Owing to strong family ties in Egypt, parents in their old age are generally well looked after by their children. Despite the fact that families in the cities are going nuclear, there is always room in such families for the grandparents. As in the past, if an elderly woman cannot look after herself, she moves in with a son or daughter. If she prefers to continue living in her own home, as such a woman often does, a grandson or close relative moves in to live with her.

However, in the case of an elderly parent who owing to various circumstances lives alone and is unable to cope with housework or have reasonable household help, a home for the elderly is a sensible alternative. This is mostly a last resort, particularly when the daughters are working or are away from home.

Until recently, homes for the elderly were state institutions for needy members of the poorer classes who had no means of sustenance and no one able to look after them. Recently, however, good quality homes for the elderly have been established, mostly by religious organizations or, in the case of elderly women, by women's associations. This arrangement took some time to be accepted by middle-class Egyptian families. They found it rather difficult to accept this alternative to caring for elderly parents, even for an elderly mother living on her own. At first the choice was made by the family, and some elderly women never took kindly to living in a home.

Gradually, the concept of a home for the elderly has become accepted by the woman herself. Not only does it relieve the daughters in particular of additional responsibilities and worries about a dear mother, but it offers better living facilities for the woman herself. In a good home, she will get service, associate with people of her own age and interests, and have nursing and medical care at hand, if needed.

Most homes are within easy reach of residential areas. Relatives and friends go to visit regularly and in case of good health, the elderly woman can be taken out for a walk, a ride or for some entertainment. Close contact with the family is always kept.

Mother-in-law, daughter-in-law

Throughout the ages, the traditional mother-in-law as matriarch was a figure more likely to be feared rather than loved. A young daughter-in-law was warned against displeasing or angering her mother-in-law. In the traditional extended family, especially in rural areas, the bride had to yield the status of mistress of the house to her husband's mother. The latter mostly held on to her authority and power. The former was obliged to accept this unfair situation. If a spirited young wife rebelled against matriarchal authority, this would most likely be the beginning of endless rows and conflicts. The poor husband was torn between wife and mother, and the situation, in extreme cases, might end in divorce.

However, this dark image of the mother-in-law represents only one side of the coin. Though she may initially feel that no woman is good enough for her son, a mother-in-law is often ready to accept the young woman of her son's choice. She may even readily accept the wife as a daughter rather than a daughter-in-law. If they share the same household, the mother-in-law might take it upon herself to initiate the young woman in her domestic duties, help with the household chores and look after the babies when they arrive. There are certainly cases of the two women being the best of friends. (*Above:* A rural grandmother taking care of her granddaughter.)

The best of friends

An amicable relationship is most likely when each of the women has her own household. The nuclear family which is the norm in urban society has contributed to a more sensible relationship between mother-in-law and daughter-in-law. So has the spread of education and employment among women. Nowadays with young mothers going to work, it is becoming customary for both mother and mother-in-law, if they are in good health and no longer working, to give a hand in looking after a small grandchild in the preschool years. The old image of the conflict between mother-in-law and daughter in-law, which often appeared in some old Egyptian films in a tragi-comic treatment, revealing the ill results of unnecessary friction, has disappeared.

Women Firsts

Sirimavo Bandaranaike	(b. 1916) She became the first woman prime minister in the world when her party, the Sri Lanka Freedom Party, won the general election in July 1960. Her husband was prime minister of Sri Lanka when he was assassinated in 1959. She led her husband's party to victory in the 1960 elections.
Sarah Breedlove	(1867–1919) Also known as Madame C.J. Walker, she was the first self-made millionairess. An uneducated African-American orphan from Louisiana, U.S.A., she founded her fortune on a hair straightener.
Nadia Comaneci	(b. 1961) The Rumanian girl was the first gymnast ever to achieve a perfect score (10.00) in the Olympic Games in Montreal in 1976. In all, she had 7 perfect scores at the Games.
Marie Curie	(1867–1934) A Polish-born French physicist, she is famous for her work on radioactivity. She was the first woman to win the Nobel Prize for Physics in 1903, together with Antoine Henri Becquerel. She was also the first woman to win the Nobel Prize for Chemistry in 1911.
Katherine Dunham	(b. 1910) American dancer, choreographer and anthropologist who was the first person to organize a black dance troupe of concert calibre, in 1940. A popular entertainer who toured the United States and Europe, she was also a serious artist intent on tracing the roots of black culture.
Amelia Earhart	(1897–?) She was one of the world's most celebrated aviators and the first woman to fly alone over the Atlantic Ocean on May 20–21, 1932. In 1935, she made a solo flight from California to Hawaii, the first person to fly this route successfully. In 1937, she set out to fly around the world with a navigator. Two-thirds through the distance, her plane disappeared in the central Pacific.
Gertrude Ederle	(b. 1906) One of the best known American sports persons of the 1920s, she was the first woman to swim the English Channel, on August 6, 1926. She swam the 35 miles from Cap Gris-Nez, France, to Dover, England, in 14 hours 31 minutes, breaking the existing men's record by 1 hour 59 minutes.
Dame Naomi James	The New Zealander is the first woman to sail round the world solo, in the cutter *Express Crusader*. She sailed from Dartmouth, England, on September 9, 1977 and reached the same port on June 8, 1978. It took her 265 sailing days to complete the journey.
Selma Lagerlöf	(1858–1940) The first woman and also the first Swedish writer to win the Nobel Prize for Literature in 1909. A novelist whose work is rooted in legend

and saga, she is said to rank among the most naturally gifted of modern storytellers.

Lucretia Mott and Elizabeth Cady Stanton

They founded the organized women's rights movment in the United States. In 1948 they organized the first Women's Rights Convention in the United States. Mott (1793–1880) also actively campaigned against slavery, and worked for voting rights and educational opportunities for freedmen after the Civil War. Stanton (1815–1902) went on to work with Susan B. Anthony for woman suffrage.

Florence Nightingale

(1820–1910) An English nurse, she was the founder of trained nursing as a profession for women. Because of the comfort and care she gave to wounded soldiers of the Crimean War (1854–) during the night rounds, she was dubbed "The Lady with the Lamp." In 1860 she established the Nightingale School for Nurses, the first of its kind in the world.

Margaret Sanger

(1883–1966) She is the founder of the birth control movement in the United States and international leader in the field. In 1916 she opened the first birth control clinic in the United States. In 1927 she organized the first World Population Conference in Geneva, Switzerland. She was the first president of the International Planned Parenthood Federation.

Junko Tabei

(b. 1939) A Japanese housewife, she was the first woman to reach the summit of Mt. Everest on May 16, 1975. She was part of the first all-woman (and all-Japanese) team to reach the summit.

Valentina V. Tereshkova

(b. 1937) A Russian cosmonaut, she was the first woman to travel in space from June 16 to 19, 1963. She was in space for 70 hours and 50 minutes. She volunteered for the cosmonaut program in 1961, and was accepted on the basis that she was an accomplished amateur parachutist, although she had no pilot training.

Baroness Bertha von Suttner

(1843–1914) An Austrian novelist and pacifist, she was the first woman to win the Nobel Prize for Peace in 1905. In 1841 she founded an Austrian pacifist organization, and from 1892 to 1899 she edited the international pacifist journal *Die Waffen nieder!* (*Lay Down Your Arms!*).

Mary Wollstonecraft

(1759–1797) An English writer and advocate of educational and social equality for women, she was the author of *A Vindication of the Rights of Women* in 1792, the first major piece of feminist writing. The book, on a woman's place in society, pleads for the illumination of woman's mind.

Glossary

al-Fatiha	First text of the Koran.
Copt	A corrupted Greek word for "Egyptian;" now refers to the Christians of Egypt.
galabia	A loose garment worn by both men and women.
governorate	Egypt is divided into 26 governorates, each headed by a governor appointed by the Prime Minister.
henna	A red dye traditionally used to color the hands and feet of the wedding couple and their close friends and relatives as a sign of jubilation.
Katb al-Kitab	The Moslem wedding ceremony, signing of the marriage contract.
mahr	Money paid to a woman as part of the marriage contract; a Moslem custom.
Mazoun	A Moslem official who officiates at the signing of the marriage contract and registers marriages and divorces.
Misr	Arabic word for Egypt.
New Valley	A reclamation project in the Western Desert which exploits underground water resources; includes the oases of Kharga, Dahkla, and Farafra.
Pasha	The highest official title of honor under the monarchy, abolished after the July 23, 1952, revolution.
Shari'a	Sacred law of Islam which defines religious duties and deals with every aspect of Moslem life.
sheikh	A learned Moslem man, generally educated at the al-Azhar Moslem University.
sherbet	Fruit squash.
The people's poet	A title given to distinguished poets.
zaghrouda	Trilling sounds made by the tongue as a sign of joy, generally made at weddings.

Further Reading

Buttles, Janet, R.: *The Queens of Egypt*, ECA Association, reprint, 1908 and 1991, Chesapeake, VA.
Langley, Andrew: *Cleopatra and the Egyptians*, Franklin Watts, New York, 1987.
Nightingale, Florence: *Letter from Egypt: A Journey on the Nile*, 1849–1850.
Sadat, Jihan: *A Woman of Egypt*, Pocket Books, New York, 1989.
Shaarawi, Huda: *Harem Years: The Memoirs of an Egyptian Feminist: 1879–1924*, Feminist Press, New York, 1987.

Fiction
Mahfouz, Naguib, *Trilogy* (in English translation): *Palace Walk* (1990), *Desire Palace* (1991), *Sugar Street* (1992), Doubleday.

Picture Credits

Index